CARD UP MY SLEEVE

Adventures of a Credit Card Smith

JAIME DOUGHSMITH

Book cover design and layout:
Ellie Augsburger of Creative Digital Studios.

Editor: Melanie M. Austin

The stories in this book reflect the author's recollection of events. Some names, locations, and identifying characteristics have been changed to protect the privacy of those depicted.

Copyright © 2015 Jaime Doughsmith

ISBN-10: 0-9969212-0-6
ISBN-13: 978-0-9969212-0-6

DEDICATION

For Delilah and Alex, without whom none of this is possible

TABLE OF CONTENTS

ACKNOWLEDGMENTS

Thanks to my editor Melanie M. Austin for the meticulous and insightful comments. The completion of this book would have been twice as long and half as fun without your advice. This book benefited in all aspects having gone through your hands.

I would also like to thank the numerous cashiers and customer service representatives who helped me buy and liquidate gift cards over the years. In this line of work it is impossible to achieve any kind of volume without having a great network of cashiers and CSRs, and I'm fortunate to have met some of the kindest and sweetest people I know behind the counters at Wal-Mart, grocery stores, and drugstores. Thanks for all the laughter, conversations, and memories. My life is richer thanks to your friendship.

THE SMITHING LIFE

"DID YOU BOOK TICKETS TO HAWAII?" my wife Delilah asked.

"I did. Two round-trip tickets to Oahu and Maui." I grinned broadly. If Hercules were to walk up to a carnival High Striker in front of his girlfriend, he'd have the same grin.

"How much did it cost?"

"Twenty-two dollars."

She barely raised an eyebrow. "Twenty-two dollars? Not bad."

The needle on my spousal impress-o-detector quivered slightly above zero. Not entirely unexpected, though. She'd been so jaded with cheap airfare that anything less than 70 percent off was cause for complaint. No matter. I had more tricks up my sleeve. "We're renting a car for the whole week."

"Oh?"

"At half the standard rate."

The needle shot up. "Not bad!"

"Plus car insurance."

"Also half off?"

I could barely suppress an ear-to-ear grin. "Nope, only $40."

"Per day? That's a bit steep, isn't it?"

"That's $40 for the whole week. Primary coverage too."

The needle nudged upwards once more, this time hovering slightly below the red critical zone. Delilah nodded appreciatively. "Good job!"

I initiated my coup de grace. "I also got travel insurance."

"Discounted too?"

"Come on. No self-respecting card master pays full price. Ever."

"Half off?"

I shook my head and jabbed an index finger downwards.

"Twenty-five percent off?"

"Totally free," I said.

The impress-o-detector went critical, and she flew into my arms. Leaning into the momentum, I picked her off the ground, and we twirled for a few timeless seconds. Stepping back, I bowed with a flourish, feeling like David Copperfield when he made the Statue of Liberty disappear. Even though my wife was familiar with the bits and pieces of my financial sleight-of-hand, she was thoroughly unacquainted with the mechanics of airline miles and credit card perks. And therein lay the magic.

Like all illusions, the effects were grand and spellbinding because they purported to break long-established and immutable laws of reality, the same laws that keep our imaginations earthbound. Besides violating the current understanding of the space-time continuum, David Copperfield broke the law of conservation of mass, the three laws of motion, federal laws against theft of public monuments, and local laws against modifying the Manhattan skyline. What I did was no less amazing from my wife's perspective. She found my financial legerdemain to be impressive because our car rental cost half the going rate and the insurance was all but free, but those were mere parlor tricks compared to the essentially free round-trip tickets to Hawaii.

Even though we live in Los Angeles, practically the closest possible mainland metropolis to Hawaii, tickets at that time of the year were going for about $400 per passenger. My round-trip tickets were the economic equivalent of pulling a rabbit out of a hat or conjuring a coin out of thin air. Adam Smith be damned; there are free lunches after all. One just has to look in the right places.

Because of the deeply subsidized airfare, we've travelled to over 30 cities in Europe in the three years after marriage. Our fondest memories, which we revisit often in the humdrum of the daily grind, include getting lost on purpose among the myriad cobblestone street and canals of Venice, going to sleep in a night train in Munich and waking up in Milan, walking through the rain in Paris under the luminous Eiffel Tower, eating Belgian waffles while sitting on the stairways of the Grand Place, watching a dancing light show in the square between the Hagia Sophia and the Blue Mosque, and taking an afternoon nap on the cobblestones in Siena's grand square. We drank too much wine for lunch in Aegina and had a grand old time finding our way back to the ferry. In Maui we sat under beach-side palm trees and watched the sun set behind the mountains of Lanai. We hiked from the Piazza de Michelangelo to the Piazza della Signoria under moonlight in Florence. When we were in Cinque Terre, we strolled the length of Via dell'Amore and got soaking wet in the waves at Monterosso al Mare. All these travels were funded through the largesse of major credit card companies although they didn't know it.

My favorite trick, which fascinates my friends to no end, is the ability to get between 3.5 and 5 percent discount on everything, including mortgages, home-owner and car insurance, property taxes, dental procedures, eyeglasses, college tuition, and student loan payments. So long as I pay a bill any way other than cash, corporate banks are providing an average discount of about 4.25 percent. When my friend had a $3,000 property tax bill to pay, I was the one he called. Back when another friend needed to book a company-reimbursable business trip to Edinburgh, he enlisted my card. The trip cost $3,500, and we split the $175 profit. Best of all, these discounts were accessible from a single debit card.

My greatest trick, however, involves shifting $19,000 a year from the revenue stream of Chase, American Express, Capital One, US Bank, Wells Fargo, Citibank, and other banks into my personal bank account. That's not exactly a king's ransom, but it isn't bad for a 35-hour per month hobby. And these profits are denominated not in airline miles, hotel points, or bank reward points, but in hard, honest cash. This is how the big banks have been bankrolling my travels around the world and funding a sizable part of my retirement. This grand magic is my fiscal equivalent to making the Statue of Liberty disappear, but in my case I get to keep the statue.

Like all illusions, my financial sleight-of-hands relies on a few basic and mundane components: a dose of financial street smarts, a pinch of discipline, some legwork and elbow grease, and a lot of time honing my craft. The miles and dollars do not materialize out of thin air. I gain them by spending over half a million dollars per year on credit cards through a hobby I call *credit card smithing*.

Defined roughly, credit card smithing is the art of refining perks and incentives from credit cards, the mainstay of which are sign-up bonuses and cashback. You've probably heard of them: 50,000 miles worth of sign-up bonuses for spending a few thousand dollars within three months of signing up, 5 percent cashback at grocery and office supply stores, free nights at large hotels for holding a chain-affiliated card, free entry into airport lounges, etc. We card smiths simply take the perks to free-market extremes. It's a deep and secretive art. My subspecialty within the field is manufactured spending, which involves making purchases on credit cards and then transferring the purchases back into funds with which to cover the credit card balances. Imagine it as playing a slot machine with a coin to which a string has been attached. Popular manufactured spending instruments include gift cards and cash reload cards, though there are plenty of other avenues for helping the purchase funds complete the circuit. The money is cycled from credit cards onto gift cards and back onto the credit cards, but the credit card rewards are mine to keep.

I consider myself a journeyman or a minor-league player at best in the game of money shuffling. The monetary shenanigans I describe in the following chapters might seem like tall tales, but they're mostly child's play compared to the feats of the big-league players. Truly, there are many card smiths who are so much greater that I'm not even worthy of loosening their sandals. I cycle $50,000 through my credit cards per month, but others (my brother being one) easily push $100,000 or more per month. I consider manufactured spending to be a hobby. Others read books, work on cars, listen to music, or craft to unwind; I smith money from credit cards. However, plenty of people work at card smithing on a part-time or even full-time basis. Comparing my records to these heavy hitters would be akin to comparing the feats of an Olympic weight lifter to Hercules' Twelve Labors.

This book is an account of my travels through the landscape of manufactured spending. When I first set out on the journey, I was a personal finance novice, but eventually I became a card master for whom a credit score is a weaponizable asset. Most of the important secrets are here. The veteran card smiths who read this book might take offense to these tales of the tools and techniques of the trade. They might object to my revealing the inner secrets of credit card arbitrage: churning credit cards, cashback portals, using airline miles for domestic and international flights, app-o-rama, leveraging bank loyalty points, buying gift cards and "feeding the birds" at Wal-Mart. But they will know that I'm not lying. I tell these tales so others can feel what it's like to be on the winning side of the war between the banks and the masses. I'd like readers to know that being at the mercy of the banks is entirely voluntary and helplessness is only a state of mind. I will tell the tales of men and women who looked at the financial institutions and saw that the system was a mug's game. Instead of refusing to play, they decided to game the system.

I'll show you an economic niche that is hidden in the shadow of credit card companies, a land on the periphery of our economic consciousness, obscured in the constant din of the battle between the credit card companies and the teeming millions. The lay of the land is littered with bones of those who have fallen to the siren call of easy credit; but the sure footed and determined can make—and have been making—a good living from the blasted lands. Where some might see only a landscape riddled with traps and pitfalls, the disciplined see a land overflowing with milk and honey. A good friend of mine describes the credit system as pitcher plant economics. By that he meant that the card corporations are carnivorous plants with pitfall traps consisting of a pool of sweet nectar at the bottom of pitcher-shaped leaves. Attracted by the nectar, ants and insects venture into the leaves. Those that lose their footings on the slippery slopes become substance for the plant. Species that can reliably navigate the treacherous terrain, however, are blessed with as much nectar as they can carry. We card smiths are that species.

One last word before we dive in. These techniques, though perfectly legal, are dangerous and potentially ruinous for the uninitiated. While the profit potential is high, so is the risk. More than once I've been accused of money laundering, but the only time I laundered money was when I forgot a gift card in the washing machine. Money laundering is the act of "washing" illicit proceeds by funneling them into ostensibly legitimate assets. It's a one-way street for the funds and a one-way ticket to the slammer if the money launderer is caught. Card smiths, on the other hand, borrow money from big banks for a few days or a few weeks, and then hand back every cent. The money we borrow is clean to begin with, and it remains so when we return it. There are many things to fear in shuffling money around, but legal threat is the one thing that never clouds the minds of card smiths. Despite what card companies might claim, there's nothing illegal in buying a gift card and using it to pay off a credit card.

The real danger of the profession lies in the risk of gift card security breaches, sudden shifts in the liquidation avenues, and card account closures. Complications constantly trouble the lives of card smiths. While the unprepared can easily (and often) find themselves stranded up fecal matter creek without a paddle, not even the wise can avoid all problems. My brother, who inducted me into the world of money cycling, once found himself stuck with $14,000 in gift cards that he could not immediately convert into cash because a popular liquidation avenue dried up overnight. He was eventually able to cycle that money back into his bank account, but it took two months. I myself had thousands of dollars tied up a few times, and had plenty of near misses involving cash registers, card activation, or unauthorized purchases. One time I had $6,000 worth of gift cards compromised, and three whole months elapsed before I saw the money again.

Tales abound in the smithing world of people who had thousands of dollars tied up for several months. It's important to remember this adage: "Don't join the fun if you can't float the funds." Even worse, it is possible to lose thousands of dollars permanently if a person does not know what he is doing.

You have been warned.

SMITHING CLANS

AS A GROUP, THE CREDIT CARD smiths, especially the manufactured spenders, are secretive, money-pinching, calculating, and not above bending a few rules for expediency. This is partly why most are fairly well-off.

There is a diverse ecosystem in card smithing. The niches and specializations are plentiful, allowing for almost any type of recreational or vocational need. For the most part, smiths stay in the shadow, content to earn miles, points, and cashback in relative anonymity. You may have seen one or two of them at the Wal-Mart customer service center, doing a bill pay and asking to split a single transaction into four separate payments of $500 each. You might have even seen a devotee of the art at the local grocery store or Post Office, asking for money orders and paying with either gift cards or funny-looking debit cards. You may have dined with a friend who insisted on paying for the entire meal with a credit card, and then received cash reimbursement from fellow dinners. You might even know people who constantly go on vacations, the frequency and the extravagance of which seem to be mysteriously beyond what can be reasonably supported by their income.

The demographics of our profession are diverse, but there are a few archetypes. First up are the travel hackers: the wander warriors whose packing skills are so legendary that the laws of physics are suspended inside the boundaries of their suitcases. Well-versed in the nuances and subtleties of the airline mileage programs, these frequent flyers can rattle off the hub cities of the major airlines with the ease of a sixth grader reciting the multiplication table. Their spouses or significant others would grumble and complain if they had to fly anything less than business class, and for some staying in anything less than a Sheraton is considered slumming it. Travel hackers thrive on app-o-ramas, applying for as many as 10 credit cards at a time to pad their frequent flyer accounts. If airline miles were dollars, then some of these airline aficionados would probably have enough in their frequent flyer accounts to retire or buy their own islands. They typically take extravagant vacations in business class and stay at five-star hotels, all of which are paid in airline miles and hotel points. The cost of obtaining the points and miles, when calculated in real money, might cost them about $300. Of course, the cost is trivial compared to the value gained. The art of credit card smithing here is a value-magnifier, greatly multiplying the worth of the dollars invested into vacations that only the truly rich or the truly profligate can experience.

Another fraction of the card smithing brethren are what I call elite status seekers. These are often road warriors or corporate travelers, who spend so much time travelling that they could probably declare the Road as their second home on tax returns. Because they spend months every year in a hotel, the complimentary Wi-Fi, room upgrades, access to the executive lounge and the gym, and the free bottles of water that come from *elite* status become as fundamental a need as a refrigerator or a car is to a typical American family. Likewise, they consider complimentary airfare upgrades, free checked bags, lounge access, priority check-in, and being able to board the airplane before military personnel and pregnant women reason enough to chase after airline elite status. Here, credit cards are shortcuts that allow them to earn Platinum or

Diamond status. A friend of mine who had United Premier 1K status (100,000 miles flown per year) was once stuck in San Francisco on a layover due to extreme weather. While her fellow flight mates queued anxiously at the ticketing desk for rerouting, my friend sat for two hours in the United VIP lounge. United assigned her a personal concierge who sat with her and mapped out various trajectories for reaching her destination—all in business class or better. Such dedicated and personalized service is what elite status travelers can rely on in time of difficulties on the road. Travelling in style and comfort: that's the ticket for these road warriors.

Besides the travel hackers and status seekers, there are the recreational manufactured spenders, whose goal is to make a few bucks on the side as a hobby. Although miles are a welcome bonus, these hobbyists are mostly concerned with supplementing their income with straight honest cash. The recreational manufactured spenders' philosophy is to go after slow and steady income, as exemplified by the slogan, "pigs get fat, hogs get slaughtered." Here the tools of choice are high cashback cards coupled with a few bank loyalty cards for diversity. When American Express (Amex) holds the Small Business Saturday promotion ($10 statement credit for purchases at a small business, good for up to three times), the typical manufactured spender might pull out 10 Amex cards that qualify. When Office Depot or Staples runs a promotion of $20 rebate per $200 in gift card purchases (one rebate per address), a run-of-the-mill manufactured spender might scrounge up about eight or 10 addresses for the rebate forms. As you've probably guessed, I belong squarely to this class.

At the top of the totem pole of Manufactured Spend are the heavy hitters. So massive is their presence, they can warp the finance-accounting continuum whenever they come close to a credit card. Their motto is "Go big and go home!" While they are seldom the first to arrive at any particular money-making opportunity, they are frequently the first ones to be shut down because of excessive abuse. By then they have already profited many times over that of their timid brethren and laughed all the way to the bank. Take the Amex Small Business Saturday promotion, for instance. I know of a heavy hitter who owned a small business. He scraped together 18 eligible cards and swiped them at his own cash register on the day of the promotion. He made 54 transactions of $10.01 each, earning roughly $540, minus merchant transaction fees, over the course of half an hour. My brother once applied for a credit card with a six-month 5 percent cashback promotion. He then proceeded to run a third of a million dollars through the card for an easy net profit of $12,000. In the heydays of the Old Blue Cash and its legendary unlimited 5 percent cashback, it was not unheard of for people to make high five-figure annual incomes solely from gift cards and credit cards (tax free, too). Rumor has it that in those days a manufactured spender in the Bay Area worked full-time driving up and down between San Jose and South San Francisco, stopping in at grocery stores to buy gift cards and then liquidating them at the Wal-Marts lining the landscape along the freeways. The card of choice for this fellow? Old Blue Cash. Supposedly, this heavy hitter made about $100,000 a year working only four to five days a week on his own hours. If he had wanted to do so, my brother could have quit his day job and matched this Bay Area fellow. The only reason he didn't was because the Old Blue Cash didn't last. Nothing does in this line of work.

Like all magic, the effects are impressive only if the secrets are concealed. I have friends who think that spending $50,000 per month on credit cards is on a par with running the Boston marathon under three hours, but once I tell them the tricks of the trade they'd slap their forehead and say, "I could've done that!" The paths of manufactured spending are long and never smooth, but the journey can be summarized by the following figure.

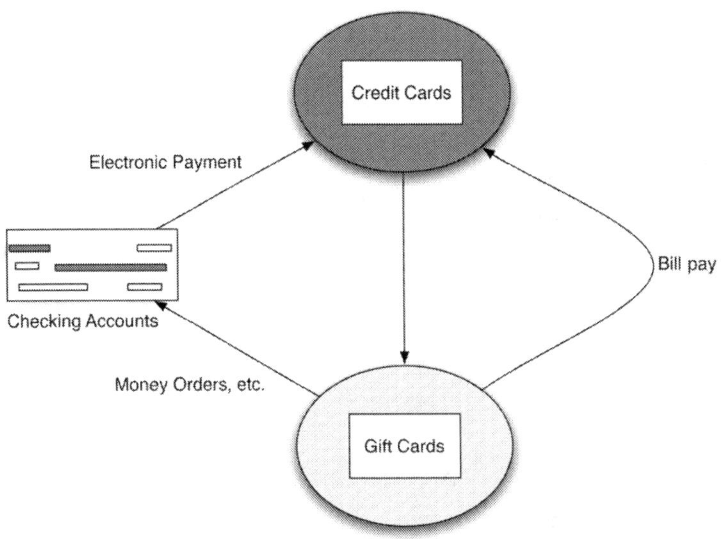

Diagram of two major manufactured spending routes

The idea is to use a credit card (preferably one with high cashback rate) and make a purchase of a cash-equivalent instrument like gift cards. Suppose that a card smith purchased a $500 gift card using a credit card. At this point he'd have a $500 debt with the credit card company and $500 trapped inside a gift card. Next, there are two major ways of funneling the funds back onto the original credit card. The first way is to use the gift cards to pay the credit cards directly. For instance, there are large retailers where one can initiate a bill pay to the credit card account and use gift card as the method of payment. Like nonstop airline flights, this way is faster and therefore preferable. The second main route requires a layover in a checking account. The main idea here is to transfer the funds from gift cards to checking accounts. For instance, the gift cards could be used at grocery stores to buy a money order. The cycle, in that case, goes as follows: credit cards → gift cards → money order → checking account → credit cards. This is but one route among many for moving money from gift cards onto checking accounts, at which point the return trip to the originating credit card is straightforward. The credit card's cashback, however, stays in the checking account as its final destination.

Those who specialize in travel hacking call their vocation the Hobby. People who chase cashback, of whom I am one, style their pursuit the Game. The credit system is the only game in town for most people, but for card smiths it's the *best* game in town.

THE WORTH OF A CREDIT SCORE

SO HOW MUCH IS A GOOD credit score worth?

A safe answer is it depends. A better answer is more than most people think.

One weekend morning I stopped by Kmart and did two bill pay with my regular cashier, Cana. The transactions were the usual $2,000 payment toward a credit card and $2,500 towards my mortgage. Usually we made mundane chit chat, but this time she took an inquisitive turn. "Why're you always paying your credit cards?"

I shot a glance at Cana and saw nothing but neighborly concern. The wrinkles on her face seemed to have been etched by forces other than time, but it remained kind.

"It's my business card," I replied. "I am paying it to maintain cash flow."

"You might want to be careful with credit cards," she said. "My daughter ran into a lot of problem with them years ago."

It was just the two of us at the customer service center. The lull in the morning right after breakfast was the best time to visit Kmart and Wal-Mart. For a small fee, both retailers allow one to make a credit card payment using a debit card. When my wife first heard of it, she asked why I bothered to make the journey to the store when I could pay credit cards and mortgage companies electronically from the comfort of home. The answer is simple. With my 3.5 percent cashback debit card, I was getting a rebate of $35 per thousand for paying at the store.

I asked for her daughter's story. Cana heaved a long sigh as she punched my credit card information into the bill-pay screen. "It wasn't just any one thing she did. She and her husband made good money, but they lived paycheck to paycheck. Their credits cards were basically a lifeline to future paychecks."

"So how did she get out of that cycle?"

"She didn't. The recession came, and she lost her job while her husband went part-time." Cana flashed a wry smile that did not remain long. The bill pay transaction continued in autopilot mode. "You seem to be a nice young man. Let me tell you a secret. Being in debt is expensive."

"Amen. I have enough student loans to buy a house in some parts of America."

She shook her head. "No, these debts are different. The further down you are the harder it is to climb out."

"But it isn't that different. You should see my monthly payment."

"At least you got an education for it. All my daughter got was a lesson."

"Did she get her life back on track?"

She shook her head sadly. "In the end, they contacted a debt negotiation company and got the balance reduced by half."

"That doesn't sound too bad."

Her face darkened. "Her credit score is ruined, though. It's been years and she still can't qualify for a mortgage."

That conversation made me think about the worth of a good credit score. Most people know what credit scores are and (generally) what to do and what not to do. Pay bills on time, maintain few inquiries, don't carry large balances, check report occasionally for errors and fraudulent activities—those are the general guidelines, and people I know tend to stick by it instinctively if not religiously.

Few people, however, are cognizant of the fact that the credit worthiness can be traded for a profit. Like most other commodities, it has a price. In theory, a credit smith could max out his credit line and declare bankruptcy, and thereby convert the credit line into liquid funds at the expense of a good score (and possibly his criminal history as well). But professionals know better than to be so wasteful. In practice, people tend to max out credit lines and then play credit card hopscotch, sending the balance from one card to another via balance transfer in hope of better days or in an attempt to delay the day of reckoning. A friend who works in the credit card settlement business tells me that in his experience the average amount of debt was between $10,000 and $15,000. These were people on the verge of destroying their credit score to rid themselves of the debts. A poor trade, it seems. To a credit card smith, that is akin to killing for meat the goose that lays golden eggs. Good creditworthiness is easily worth many times that amount if harvested non-destructively.

In a typical month, I move about $50,000 in gift cards at an average net cashback rate just a shade above 3 percent. Monthly profit comes out to be approximately $1,600 per month, though it is only a lower-bound estimate because I have yet to add in profits from benefits like free flights, deeply discounted car rentals, gift card rebates, and promotional Amex Sync Offers.

Being the numerical type, I once sat down and tried to calculate the hourly rate, but found it varies greatly among credit card smiths because it depends on the geographic locations and friendliness of cashiers. It is not unheard of for a gift card enthusiast to drive more than half an hour each way to locate a friendly Wal-Mart, and I've read of people who make weekly trips to New Jersey from New York for their gift card fix (apparently New Jersey is more tolerant of transactions of questionable character). People in the know say that this game is much easier in Southern California than in New York, though both locales are nowhere near the top of the smithing-friendly list. I consider myself lucky to have three Wal-Marts within a ten-mile radius of my home, and one of them is even right off the freeway on the way to work.

On average, I can buy and liquidate $8,000 within three and a half hours, driving time included. That breaks down to about one and a half hour for acquiring the gift cards, another one and a half for liquidating them, and half an hour for peeling the gift cards and making the proper bookkeeping updates. Seven more hours are reserved per month for the Internet-based money shuffling activities. Add in about six more hours for miscellaneous tasks like applying for airline miles, filing complaints for compromised cards, and chasing a few occasional promotions, and I'm looking at about approximately 35 hours per month devoted to money smithing. So, my monthly haul is about $1,600 per month, or approximately $45 per hour. That's how much my wife's and my credit scores are worth to us. It isn't a path to untold wealth, but it sure beats collecting stamps or clipping coupons as a hobby.

A credit score is a strange thing. Many view it as a burden and use it sparingly, if at all. Others consider it a necessary evil, the price one pays for a functional credit economy. Some people even go as far as to call a credit score, "the shackle of capitalism," and absolutely foreswear any use arising from or related to it. Some consider it a conduit to future paychecks, and yet others still view it as a font of free money that should be drained lest it goes to waste. Although a credit score can be used sparingly or even destructively, it shines brightest when used sustainably as a renewable resource. Bane or boon, encumbrance or endowment, radioactive or remunerative, it's all a matter of perspective.

The truth is it's easy to harvest money from a credit score. I'm not kidding. Financial companies are practically falling over themselves to give away money, and a good credit card smith with a few borrowed identities can make $200 per month without even putting on shoes. (You have to be careful whose identities you choose to borrow, though. The general rule of thumb is only to ask for permission from people who either share at least 50 percent of your DNA or have hospital visitation rights). Let me name an example of harvesting credit score. A friend of mine once alerted me to a certain online bank with a special checking promotion that offered a $20 bonus per month for making direct deposits totaling at least $1,500 and making use of their online bill pay service. Paycheck deposits counted towards the direct deposits requirements, but no way was I going to switch my paychecks from my Bank of America to this online bank.

After some trials and errors, I set up my online stock account to automatically withdraw $1,500 from Bank of America every month and immediately thereafter deposit the funds into this online bank. It counted as a direct deposit, and on the stock account it was set as an automated recurring transaction so no manual intervention was necessary. The bill pay requirement, unfortunately, could not be automated, so I still had to log into the checking account once per month to make two bill pays to utilities. Occasionally, the process required a check to transfer excess funds back onto the Bank of America account. This took ten minutes per month, tops. Between my wife and me, that's an easy $40 per month for 20 minutes of shuffling money around. And this was one of the harder routes for harvesting creditworthiness without putting on pants! As a wise man once said, "The harvest is plentiful, but the workers are few."

A good credit score is a terrible thing to waste.

The other day, my mother cornered me in her kitchen when I came to visit. "Your brother Harry was here the other day. I owed his wife $60, so I tried to return it but he refused."

"Do you want me to return the money for you?"

"Heavens no! He did something strange."

"Like what?"

"He left the house and came back half an hour later. He said he just recouped $80." She squinted her eyes. "How'd he do that?"

Not a lot of clues to go on, but I can guess it had something to do with gift cards. Either that or he went out and held up a gas station. I briefly explained the outlines of the business. He'd probably gone to a grocery store and bought $2,000 in gift cards using a 5 percent cashback card. Factor in the gift card fees, and that worked out to be exactly $80 in profit.

She did a quick mental calculation. "Credit card companies are really paying out $50 per $1,000?"

I nodded.

"How much do you and he do per month?" she asked.

"For me, $50,000, give or take. I don't know about his rake, though."

She did another calculation—she was always very good with mental gymnastics. Her eyes widened. "That's more than double what your father gets in Social Security!"

"It's true. I've been trying to convince him to join the Game."

She thought about it for a while. A stout believer in the American dream, she worked hard and uncomplainingly most of her life to support my siblings and me. In her current job she was earning the current minimum wage of $9 per hour.

"Is there a special requirement to get these cards?"

"No, just a good credit score."

"Nothing like a high income or having a house?"

"No, mother."

"Are you sure?"

"Yes, mother."

"Seriously, credit card companies give you $50 per $1,000?" she repeated.

"Yes, mother."

"Are they stupid?"

Ah, one of the harder questions in life.

BEFORE THE GOLDEN AGE

AS LONG AS CREDIT SCORES HAVE existed, card smiths have been busy at harvest. Manufactured spending arose as soon as credit cards came into form, and its history could be divided roughly into a sequence of ages. At the time of this writing, manufactured spending is in the twilight of the Golden Age—the time of Wal-Mart and debit gift cards. This age started on April 1, 2013, when gift card issuers added a secondary debit network to prepaid cards, in accordance with the Durbin Amendment of the Dodd-Frank Act (2010). In effect, Dodd-Frank forced gift card providers to allow gift cards to run as a debit transaction, in addition to the standard credit transaction.

This change ushered in a new age of prosperity for card smiths because not all card transactions are created equal. In general, electronic payment can be either debit or credit, and the difference between them can be encapsulated in the concept of *pay now* versus *pay later*. In a debit payment the customer withdraws money from his or her checking account, and the card processor serves as an intermediary for the immediate transfer of funds from the debit card into the merchant's account. Because you always have to enter a PIN when doing a debit, once the transaction is completed, the funds are as good as gone. This payment type is just like cash: you can't spend more than you have.

In a credit card transaction there's an extra entity in the middle. When the customer signs the payment screen, he or she is essentially borrowing money from a bank (the credit card issuer) to pay for the purchase. The bank then pays the merchant, and the customer pays the bank back at the end of the month when the card statement closes. Credit cards allow purchases up to a fixed limit called credit line, which may or may not be commensurate with the cardholder's actual ability to pay.

From the merchant's point of view, debit transactions are almost as good as cash since they receive the funds immediately, while the credit transactions are only as good as the signature on the payment slip. In fact, merchants hold them in higher regards than checks because unlike checks debit transactions will not "bounce." This is why certain grocery stores allow the option of *in-store cash back*. Not to be confused with credit card cashback, in-store cash back refers to the practice of adding a stipulated amount (typically up to $50) to the purchase price and receiving the difference in cash when using a debit card. Likewise, most cash-equivalent transactions like payments on student loans or property taxes, money orders, and bill pay require debit cards for electronic payment. Gift cards used to be processed solely as credit, and you can imagine the exuberance of card smiths everywhere when gift cards were allowed to run as debit transactions because of the Dodd-Frank Act. It made possible the workflow that all cards smiths know and love: credit cards → gift cards → money order or cash equivalent → credit cards.

I joined late in the Golden Age of manufactured spending and was inducted into card smithing halfway in the epoch when some of the most lucrative and legendary deals of the age were already dead. Before this age was the Silver Age, which started in 2008 when the US Mint started selling $1 coins at face value with no shipping fee. That was an era when men with ingenuity and strong back muscles were harvesting money and loyalty points from the US Mint with abandon.

In the years before the Silver Age, the art of manufactured spending was still in its infancy, though there were still plenty of opportunities for profiting from airlines and hotel promotions. Those opportunities, however, are mostly unrecorded and mostly lost to time. I call that time the Prehistoric Era. Though still profitable, this era lacked an age-defining blockbuster like the Mint or, eventually, Wal-Mart and debit gift cards.

Shuffling money in those days included methods such as the time-tested checking-account opening, in which a card smith opens a checking account and uses a credit card to fund the initial deposit. Apparently banks are so desperate for new deposit accounts that they happily absorb the credit card fee in return for the privilege of holding onto the customer's funds. The savvy smith would then hold the deposit in the bank for a few months and then withdraw and pay back the credit card. This venue becomes much more attractive when combined with checking promotions. For instance, one bank used to offer a limited-time promotion of $300 for opening a checking account and making three direct deposits. It is fairly easy to meet the direct deposit requirement, since any good credit smith knows that electronic withdrawals from stock accounts such as Vanguard, Scottrade, and Fidelity count as direct deposits.

Yet another way for cycling money through credit cards in the old days was the good old buy-and-rebate. Certain stores, in particular office supplies and electronic, tend to have free-after-rebate offers. In this scenario, a card smith might buy a $100 printer that has a rebate offer for the exact value. After submitting the rebate form, he or she would receive a check for the purchase price, thus completing the card's spending requirement. In addition, the buyer can then sell the printer through Craigslist or eBay for reasonably good profits.

Of course, this method was not limited to free-after-rebate items. Certain items might have high enough resale value that even a partial rebate—say, a $50 rebate on an $80 item—would be profitable. Software in general was the favorite medium of the rebate hustler. Software programs often come in small light packages, much more portable than, say, a printer at the same price. Furthermore, certain software, such as antivirus programs, is often priced high, making it particularly profitable for credit card perks. In the later years, card smiths discovered that it was possible to buy these free-after-rebate items online through a shopping portal, which gave an additional discount as a sort of referral. For instance, a shopping portal such as Topcashback would offer 5 percent cashback for any purchase made at Staples through its affiliate link. Card smith would go to Topcashback.com and click on the 5 percent cashback Staples link, which directed them to staples.com. There, he would buy a free-after-rebate item worth, say, $100 using a Chase Ink Bold credit card, which gave an additional 5 percent cashback. His total profit would be $5 from Chase, $5 from the shopping portal, and perhaps $30 from reselling the rebate item.

A variant of the technique above is the famous buy-and-return method, in which a customer buys an item using a credit card and then exploits a loophole or oversight on the merchant's part to get a refund in cash. A famous example of this was the Costco return rush in 2013. At that particular time, Costco only accepted American Express cards in their brick-and-mortar stores. However, the online version of the store (costco.com) accepted Visa and MasterCard in addition to American Express. Since the physical stores did not accept Visa, they had no means to return the funds electronically onto the Visa card, and therefore had to resort to either cash or check. Investigative card smiths soon found that one could buy a high-value item, such as a $10,000 engagement ring, at Costco online using a Visa card, and then return it to the brick-and-mortar store. I can imagine what people stated as the reason for returning the ring: "I'd like to return this engagement ring. My girlfriend didn't accept my marriage proposal."

Eventually Costco caught on to the abuse and started requiring diamond jewelry above one carat to be returned to Costco Online offices so that the original credit card could be credited. Card smiths then side-stepped the limitation by branching out into other high-value items. Favorite choices included portable items such as laptops, tablets, phones, and fashion accessories—it just didn't make sense to order non-portable items like a $3,000 mattress if one needed to schlep it into Costco for return. For the intrepid card smith, there was the $30,999.99 Breitling Windrider Gold Watch ("Excuse me, I'd like to return this $30,000 watch. Oh, there's nothing wrong with it. At that price, I thought the watch could bring back the dead and reverse entropy, but it could only raise the dead.") Costco grew tired of receiving more returns than a tennis player facing Rafael Nadal on clay and closed the loophole in late 2013. The practice still lives on today in certain necks of the retailing woods, though to protect the innocent I will not name names.

In western mythology, we have stories of Theseus slaying the Minotaur, Perseus petrifying the sea serpent to save Andromeda, and Hercules diverting rivers to clean the Augean stables. Likewise, in the world of cards and miles we have stories of heroes who by dint of acuity managed to score substantial profits, and for that they are remembered for their exploits. There's the story of the Mr. Pickles (a nom de guerre) who ordered over $800,000 in $1 coins from the Mint over the span of three years. Another story tells of a nameless hero who took advantage of Chase Freedom's 10 points per transaction promotion by automating 10,000 Amazon one-cent gift purchases to clean up to the tune of 100,000 Chase Ultimate Rewards points. Yet another tale describes how travel-hacking legend Steve Belkin once hired 20 Thai rice farmers to fly four times a day for six whole weeks between the cities of Chang Mai and Chang Rai to rack up frequent flyer miles. Another story depicts a pair of brothers who flew too close to the sun, bilking Nordstrom out of 1.4 million dollars in cashback, and eventually fell to ruinous ends. And there's the story of the pudding guy, who took advantage of a Healthy Choice pudding promotion to earn 1.2 million miles (valued at probably $25,000) for an out-of-pocket cost of about $3,000. The last story is probably most well-known, not for the sheer amount of profit, but rather for the ingenuity and the outlandish vehicles for acquiring the miles.

In May of 1999, David Phillips, a self-professed travel aficionado and miles collector extraordinaire, saw a promotion from frozen food manufacturer Healthy Choice for 500 airline miles for any purchase of 10 Healthy Choice frozen entrees. The consumer would have to send in the barcodes to qualify for the miles, and there was a double point bonus for sending them in the first month of the promotion. At that time, airline miles were probably valued at two cents per points, making this early bird special offer equivalent to $20 for every 10 barcodes sent in.

Upon catching news of the promotion, David reconnoitered the local supermarkets to assess the price of all the Healthy Choice frozen entrees that qualified for the airline miles. His goal was to look for the cheapest frozen entrees, and he found the vehicle of choice in the frozen puddings. Grocery Outlet, a grocery chain that specialized in selling excess inventory to consumers at a discount, was selling the individual pudding cups for 25 cents each. Doing the math, he quickly realized that 10 puddings would cost him $2.50, but those would net him 1,000 airline miles, which were worth $20—a rate of return on investment that only loan sharks or elected officials manage to achieve. For the next few days, David set out to buy all the puddings at the grocery stores within the region, cleaning up every single shelf and asking the employees for all the stocks in the backroom. He got a list of regional Grocery Outlet locations from the store manager—this being the time before Google Maps—and drove with his mother-in-law between Davis and Fresno for the frozen desserts (you know what they say, behind every successful man there's a surprised mother-in-law). He eventually had a special order through the Grocery Outlet store manager in his hometown for 60 cases of pudding, which he picked up at the store via the back entrance. Naturally, quite a few people were suspicious of the strange white-collared gentleman buying up all the puddings, and he quelled their suspicion saying that he was preparing for Y2K, which was only six months away.

After about $3,038 in spending, David acquired 12,150 cups of pudding, which he stacked floor-to-ceiling in his garage and home. He then had the unglamorous task of peeling the barcodes from the puddings and sending them in. His family, neighbors, and coworkers tired of the chocolate puddings that he was forcing on them, and his wife and kids got blisters from peeling hundreds of stickers from the packing. The month of

May was ending, and the deadline for the early bird double point promotion loomed. It seemed doubtful that his family had enough time and fresh fingers to peel off and send in all the barcodes.

Once again, David had a great idea, demonstrating an acuity that separated him from his mere mortal deal-seeking brethren. He contacted the local charity food banks and offered to donate the boatload of puddings in his garage in exchange for having the charity workers peeling the UPC codes off and returning them to him afterwards. The charities served puddings for breakfast, lunch, and dinners to diners who had no idea that their desserts were fulfilling the dreams of a man to see the world, and soon David was in possession of 12,150 barcodes, which he sent off to Healthy Choice and crossed his fingers, hoping for the best. Under the terms of the promotion, the frozen puddings qualified for the free miles, though there was a very real possibility that Healthy Choice might disqualify him on some technicality. However, within a few weeks packages in various shapes and sizes arrived, containing certificates that were each good for 500 miles. In all, he received 2,506 certificates, which were good for a total of 1,253,000 miles.

David eventually chose to deposit over one million of his miles in American Airline program. At the time, American Airlines was offering lifetime American Airlines Advantage Gold status to persons with over one million miles in their account, regardless of the miles' provenance. David's miles earned him Gold status, which conferred special privileges, including priority boarding, upgrades, dedicated help lines, additional flight bonus miles, and lifetime bragging rights among travel hackers and manufactured spenders alike. In economy class, his miles were worth 31 round-trip tickets to

Europe, 42 tickets to Hawaii, 21 tickets to Australia, or 50 tickets to anywhere within the United States.

When this story is told on the Internet, a popular addendum says that David claimed the $3,038 pudding purchase as a charitable donation, allowing him to get about $815 in tax deduction at the end of the year and bringing his total cost down to about $2,223 for the 1.2 million miles. I have my doubts. No one, and I mean *no* one, beats the Tax Man without being crooked or extremely wealthy. Those 1,215,000 miles fall squarely under the category of award, prizes, or contest winnings, and were supposed to be reported under miscellaneous income. If he counted the pudding as charitable deductions, then he'd have to report the miscellaneous income as well. At his tax rate, the tax liabilities of the extra income would have more than wiped off the benefits of the charitable deduction. The gaze of the IRS is a lot like the Eyes of Sauron—you never want it trained on you whether you're sneaking on the slopes of Mount Doom or making money pushing puddings.

The Silver Age started in 2008, when the US Mint offered free shipping and handling on presidential and Native American $1 coins, which were sold at face value direct to the consumers. Initiated in 2005 as part of the Presidential $1 Coin Program that sought to put dollar coins into circulation, the Mint officially started selling the coins in 2007, but sales of the coins didn't take off until 2008. The reason this method was so beloved of card smiths was because the Mint accepted all major credit cards for purchase, and ordering was conveniently done online. It didn't take long for airline miles enthusiasts and credit card warriors to realize that they could buy the coins from the comfort of home using a credit card, deposit the coins at a bank, and use the funds to pay the credit card, while gaining free points like a basketball team with a crooked referee in its pocket. This was the Holy Grail of manufactured spending. To this day the deal (lovingly referred to as the *Mint*) is enshrined in the memory of every manufactured spender as the gold standard to which every other worthwhile opportunity is compared. To some, it was the ideal manufactured spending venue, the Platonic form compared to which all other posterior opportunities are but mere imperfect shadows.

By the time that the deal was cancelled in 2011, 130 million coins had been sold to 40,000 unique collectors, according to the US Mint. In my experience, many of these promotions conform to the Pareto principle, otherwise known as the 80–20 rule, which states that for many events 80 percent of the effects come from 20 percent of the causes. A famous example is the distribution of the world's wealth in which 20 percent of the world's richest earned 80 percent of the world's income. In the case of the Mint, I would conjecture that 20 percent of the collectors (8,000) ordered 80 percent of the coins (104 million). I am sure that the 8,000 top collectors were card smiths, every single last one of them. Who else would order tens of thousands of $1 coins?

The Mint came about as the harmonic convergence of market inefficiency and the law of unintended consequences, creating the manufactured spending dream deal, the likes of which probably will never come again. Several factors forever enshrined the Mint among the constellation of all-time greats: credit cards acceptance, no fees, scalability, and free shipping. The fact that the Mint accepted credit cards and that there was no hard limit on volume (called *scalability* in smithing parlance) made this deal phenomenal. The lack of fees pushed it further toward transcendental, but the free shipping was what made the deal legendary. The Mint made it possible to cycle money with no cost besides the time required for ordering, picking-up, and depositing.

The mechanics of the deal were straight forward. One could order the coins online, and the coins came in $250 boxes (ten rolls of $25 each). Each box weighed an astounding 4.5 lbs with packaging, so $2,000 in these coins would have weighed 36 lbs, the same as a completely full five-gallon water bottle! Shipping for large purchases was expedited via UPS Next Day Air or Priority Mail, and packages required a signature upon delivery, with no exception. Some card smiths had busy schedules that prevented signing for delivery at home, so they would drive to the UPS store on weekends and back their trucks directly onto the loading dock to load the boxes of coins, which they then deposited at their local banks. Others would sign for the UPS delivery at home, and then have the postman plunk the coin package directly into their car's trunk. Most banks did not require the coins to be unrolled, though the package did need to be opened. Once the coins were deposited into their checking account, card smiths would pay their credit cards and repeat the cycle anew.

I missed the Mint entirely. Whenever I think about this event, I feel like a Californian who went on a whaling trip in 1848 and missed the entire San Francisco Gold Rush. Sometimes I wonder what card I would have used if I had been present at the time of the Mint. From my research, it seemed that there were three main routes to generate profit. The first was to apply for massive number of cards every three months, a practice lovingly known as *app-o-rama*, and then to use the Mint for meeting spending requirements. A round of app-o-rama might include two to 10 cards, which included a mix of hotels (Mariott, Hyatt, etc.) and airlines (Delta, American,

United, Hawaiian, etc.), though occasionally cards with large bank-loyalty points (Chase Ultimate Rewards or American Express Membership Rewards) might be thrown in for good measure. At roughly $1,000 minimum spending per card, that worked out to be $2,000 to $10,000 in spending every three months, which was fairly doable even without relying on the Mint. At an estimate of $300 rewards per card, the profit from such an app-o-rama might range from $600 to $3,000. In terms of the amount of spending required versus rewards, these sign-up bonuses are in a league of their own. I suspect that these credit card churners got the best bang for the buck for their time on the Mint.

Another approach was to use the legendary Starwood's Preferred Guest (SPG) card for ordering from the Mint. This card was popular because it had good redemption rates at Starwood Hotel properties, which included brands such as Westin, Sheraton, and Four Points. But what made it truly great was that these points were transferable to some key airline frequent flyer programs, such as American Airlines, British Airways, and Japan Airlines at a rate of 1.25 miles per SPG point. An article I read claimed that one heavy hitter ordered two million dollars from the Mint through his SPG card, which he then transferred into American Airlines AAdvantage points, which thereby granted him lifetime Platinum status. That's one level up from the Gold status David earned from the pudding deal. At a conservative estimate of two cents per SPG point, his haul from the Mint was $40,000. I envy him the miles, but I sure don't envy the work of schlepping the 40,000 pounds of coin to the bank.

The last avenue for generating profit was to use a cashback credit card, the most standard of which was the ubiquitous 2 percent cashback. At an average rate of $10,000 per month (only 200 lbs of coins), one could make $200 per month. By switching to the Citi Platinum, which gave 3 percent cashback if redeemed for student loans, one could make $300 on the same amount of work. The best card, however, came a bit late in the game when the deal was in its twilight. In early 2011 at the height of the cashback craze, Chase introduced a cobranded American Association of Retired Persons (AARP) credit card that gave 5 percent cashback on everything within six months of the card's opening. Needless to say, manufactured spenders jumped on the card like lions ambushing a gazelle in the Serengeti.

Soon after the start of the program, Treasury officials noticed a large uptick in the number of repeat orders and the strange fact that the majority of buyers were individuals as opposed to businesses or institutional customers. At the same time, they were receiving notice from banks around country of large deposits of $1 coins, some still in their US Mint packaging. A search of the Internet revealed online forums where the details were specified in minute details including package carriers, the recommended credit cards, and the deposit strategy. Thereafter the Mint engaged in a cat-and-mouse game with the so-called abusers. They would limit the amount of coins per name and address, and in response the card smiths would enlist the help of family, friends, authorized user cards, slightly misspelled addresses, different choices of honorifics, and so on in an attempt to thwart the ordering cap. Eventually, in June of 2011, the US Mint threw in the towel and disabled credit cards as a payment option for the coins, thus ending the Silver Age of manufactured spending.

In their statement, the US Mint said it could no longer accept credit cards for $1 coins because of "individuals purchasing $1 coins with credit cards, accumulating frequent flyer miles, and then returning coins to local banks." They went on to explain that "While not illegal, this activity was a clear abuse and misuse of the program."

Not illegal, yet clear abuse. Private-sector card corporations have been saying the same thing of card smiths for years, though in their case it's the pot calling the kettle black.

GROWING UP

MOVING $50,000 OF GIFT CARDS PER month can appear effortless—a financial version of what the Italian called *sprezzatura,* or studied carelessness. It wasn't always that way, though. I grew up during the smithing prehistoric era with absolutely no clue about personal finance and money management. No one taught me basic financial literacy. My parents never got around to teaching it, and my high school didn't offer a course in it, both of which I now consider gross oversights. It was only by a stroke of luck that I didn't fall into the downward spiral of credit card debt.

Growing up, my family was poor. We were not poor as in penniless, impoverished, indigent, in-constant-danger-of-being-evicted or stretching-a-pot-of-bean-to-last-the-entire-week poor. My family could afford a two-bedroom apartment, though we had to split the rent with another family, whose son was my childhood best friend. There were 10 of us in that 1,500 square-foot unit. Five of us boys occupied the largest room. As the youngest lad, I had the privilege of sleeping on the floor in the closet, where I had a sliding door to give me some semblance of privacy and ownership, though in retrospect those benefits were more symbolic than functional. At night, the room transformed into a warzone with futons and sleeping mats haphazardly strewn across the floor, arms and legs of sleeping boys thrown about in somnambulant disarray. Downstairs, my mother and father slept in a bed strategically placed behind the sofa. My sister, poor thing, called the empty space beneath the stairs her room, which was demarcated from the rest of the room by a curtain fastened to the side of the railing.

Summers were unbearably hot. My family never used air conditioning. We knew where the AC knob was and what it did, but it got as much use as a drum kit in Anne Frank's hideaway. I remember tossing on the paper tile floor of the closet on hot summer nights, turning in my sleep so that my exposed arms and legs could find a cool region of paper tile and for a few brief moments enjoy respite from the oppressive heat. The coolness would soon evaporate, leaving behind a sweaty stickiness between the skin and the tile floor, and I had to agitate again in search of untouched floor.

I didn't have any allowance as a kid. My only source of money came on Christmas, New Year, and my birthday when my parents and older brothers gave me money, the most pragmatic gift possible. I wanted the money, and gifting money involved less work on the part of the giver. Whenever my birthday rolled around, I parked myself right in the living room sofa and watched TV while waiting for my older brothers to get home. When one of them walked in the front door, I would say casually, "Hello brother, my birthday is today," as if it was the most matter-of-fact thing in the whole world. They would invariably have a surprised look on their face as if they were Custer's men hearing Indian battle whoops at Little Horn, but being caught they would mumble Happy Birthday, dig into their pockets, and give me whatever change they had.

The majority of the windfall ended up in toys and video games. By the time junior high rolled around my family was slightly better off, and instead of 10 people the two-bedroom apartment only had to house seven. My parents were able to afford a Super Nintendo for my brother Ben and me. On the night before buying the console system I woke up several times before dawn, each time hoping that sunrise would come earlier, so that I could wake my parents to go to the store. It was of the longest night, the likes of which I only experienced on the nights before the SAT and my wedding (I'm not kidding). When I did get the Super Nintendo system, I spent many happy hours of my childhood on the sofa fighting monsters, exploring worlds, saving princesses, leveling up heroes, and defeating red-robed communist street fighters. I'm sure my IQ permanently dropped 10 points from all those hours glued to the console, but I have no regrets.

When newer generation consoles came out, my parents couldn't afford the pricy Nintendo 64 and PlayStation, so I entertained myself by walking a mile and a half to the nearest Best Buy, which had the new consoles on display. There I would play whatever game they had, though two-player games such as Super Mario Kart or Smash Bros were my favorites. The display panels had two controllers, and the store patrons, mostly kids, abided by the winner-stay, loser-leave rules. At around four or five in the evening, neighborhood kids crowded the console display, waiting for their turn in a snaking queue. The neighborhood kids all knew each other, and there was a pecking order for each game, established by the gaming virtuosity of each participant. Some kids were generalists, quick to learn new games and to hone their skills to virtuoso levels. And then there were the specialists who were generally average players, but were like Rain Man when it came to their area of expertise. I was particularly adept at racing games. The objective of racing around a circular track in the least possible amount of time always resonated strongly with me. Those timed laps were a competition against each other as well as against oneself. Even when I came in first, there was always the drive to repeat a course, tighten a turn, or cut a corner to shave a few more seconds off the completion time. In that circle, I was known as the Kart Kid, a reference to the game Nintendo racing game Mario Kart. When that game was on display, I was like Manny Pacquiao—scrawny, lightning fast, and (mostly) unbeatable.

My parents did send me to Boy Scouts, which met every Sunday in the shaded grove of a neighborhood park across from a small church. Next to the grove was a basketball court, where in the evening youngsters, hipsters, and gangsters gathered to shoot hoops or shoot the breeze. It wasn't a neighborhood where I'd want to raise my kid, but it wasn't so bad growing up in it. The unofficial neighborhood rule was that as long as you don't bother anybody, then nobody would bother you. In my later days in Scouts, I liked to walk to the basketball court after the troop meeting and observe the basketball games. It was a poor man's version of people watching.

I remember walking to my favorite bench on the side of the court one evening and seeing the basketball courts less crowded than usual. Instead, the usual crowd huddled in one corner of the court where someone had put down a poster-sized piece of canvas. It was a gambling game of some sort. Rude lines divided the canvas into a three-by-two grid, and in each square was drawn a number that went from one to six.

The operator was a swarthy man with wearing a cap with the visor backwards. He wore a pager on his belt, and his hair was combed backwards in slick oleaginous rows. Every once in a while he hollered, "Come one, come all. No bet is too large, no bet is too small. Can't win big if you don't play!"

I sat on the bench watching the game for a few minutes and got the gist of the rules. It was straightforward. The operator held a small bowl with three dice. After the bets were put down, he'd shake and bowl and then, glibly bantering, open it with great ceremony. You get paid the amount of your bet for each time a dice show the number of your bet. If your number showed on one die, you get your money back plus one times your bet. If your number showed on three dice, then your winning was the original bet plus three times the money.

The thin throng immediately surrounding the operator consisted of a few active players and a smattering of observers. Some of the latter watched the game intently with their arms folded, others lounged about feigning disinterest with hands coolly tucked into pockets. From this crowd one kid stepped up, flanked on either side by friends, and casually slapped down a bet that sent a ripple through the canvas. One fellow on his side slapped him on the back. "Thirty dollars! Baller got balls!"

The operator picked up the bowl of dice and proffered it to the young baller. He blew on it earnestly. A few quick shakes and the operator slapped the bowl down. Lifting up one corner, the operator gingerly peeked in while taking care not to disturb the contents. He slapped his hands down in theatrical disgust. "Damn it!" He uncovered the bowl and a crowd broke into a wild whoop. The young baller did a fist pump while his friends rushed him in congratulations and applause. Handshakes and backslaps went all around in an abundance of exuberance.

The operator licked his fingers and counted through the thick billfold in his hand. "Today isn't my day. Two dice showing his number! That's a cool $60 I'm not seeing again anytime soon." He held the payout up at head level and looked around like a man vindicated. "See that fellas? Can't win big if you don't play."

From the bench I emptied my pockets. The contents therein consisted of one dollar and one or two quarters. I stared at them intently. He'd said no bet was too small.

"Fancy a turn at the table?"

I looked up into the eyes of my assistant troop leader Gary. His lips were smiling but his eyes weren't. I could feel blood rushing to my cheeks. I wasn't quite caught red-handed, but he sure caught me red-faced. "N-no, sir."

He sat down next to me and lit up a cigarette. He was a wiry fellow with rubbery skin and hard eyes. Although he was younger than my father was, there were already patches of white hair on the side of his temples. In the scouting session he deferred mostly to the troop leader and never talked much. He blew out a long puff of smoke. The wind caught the smoke and blew it towards me in a haze. He smiled apologetically while holding up the cigarette pinched between his index and middle fingers.

"They say there are four vices in life. I've tried them all, and this is the only one my wife lets me keep." He pointed the cigarette, the embers still glowing red, in the direction of crowd. "Don't bother unless you want to throw your money away."

I said nothing but continued staring at the baller who just won big. He'd reinvested his winning into game with enthusiasm. Gary followed my gaze. "Sixty dollars, that's a lot of money, isn't it Jaime?"

"Yes, sir."

"Seems like an innocent game, right?"

"Yes, sir."

"Scouting's over. You don't have to call me 'sir'." He shook his head and lowered his voice. "There's nothing but cheats in this game. Look at man with the dice. Do you see anything strange?"

I squinted and followed the operator's movements. "I don't see anything."

"See how he taps the dice after all the money is put down?"

"Yes."

"It means he's not leaving anything to chance."

He leaned back and puffed on the cigarette. I didn't quite understand how it worked, but I'd watched enough movies to get the gist of it. I continued observing the game, but now in the capacity of a disinterested spectator instead of a hopeful participant. The billfold in the operator's hand indeed seemed to grow consistently larger. The young baller continued playing, but judging by the dour intensity on his face his earlier winnings had already evaporated.

Gary suddenly gave a chuckle, spewing out a tiny cloud of smoke as he did so. "Not bad. The thief has met an old lady."

I followed his gaze and found a young fellow off to the side canvas. He wore glasses and stood by himself. Unlike his fellow players, he was somewhat disengaged from the game. An air of aloofness disconnected him from the intensity of everyone else.

"See how he is always the last one to make the bet?"

"Yes, sir."

"Look closely. He's only putting money on the number with the smallest total bet."

"Um . . . I don't get it."

"It means he's not leaving anything to chance neither."

I still didn't quite get the last part, though I understood that somehow it enabled the fellow to "win" at this game. "If I do what he does can I win too?"

"No, everyone loses in the end. The only way to win is not to play."

***

I spent my childhood mostly untroubled by money. Most families in the neighborhood were in the same economic situation; thus their kids were similarly unaccustomed to displays of wealth, let alone its flashier side. Mostly, we had fun because no one told us money was necessary to have fun. Surrounded by kids of like status, I rarely felt the privation of being poor, but occasionally the reminders would creep in. I didn't mind so much the lack of money or comfort; it was the appearance of being poor that I terribly dreaded. One such instance was when I was around 11 and a travelling barber wandered through the neighborhood. My parents, being the economical kind, availed of his service and he set up shop in front of my door, smack in the middle of the neighborhood walk way. My parents brought a chair outside, and I was unceremoniously perched on the chair, wrapped in a barber cape while this stranger hovered and clipped my hair. All my neighbor friends were outside playing, and they all seemed to be stealing a glance or two of either pity or mockery in my direction. Looking back through the lens of adulthood, my friends were likely amused at the whole spectacle, but at that moment I was sure they were judging me, their every glance burning a crimson blush on my cheeks. That's not to mention that the girl I liked at the time, a lithe young girl with a cute ponytail, stood off in the distance fixedly gazing at me. With every cut, my hair clippings fell into the wind and dispersed like dark broken dandelion seeds, each filament taking along a tiny piece of my prepubescent dignity.

That was the first time I remembered feeling poor. My mother used to tell me that money can't buy love or happiness, and she was absolutely right. But she never told me that the convenience store of Life has many other things for sale. Apparently comfort, status, fun, peace of mind, and self-confidence are available for purchase next to the check-out counter.

Thankfully, once I grew up a bit more and started junior high, my parents thought the better of it and took me to a barbershop near their favorite grocery store. That certainly was much preferred over the mobile barber, but it was still an occasion of dread on a par with going to the dentist. Every time, my father would deposit me in the barbershop and inform the barber that he would be back later before going off to grocery shop. I would sit still in my seat while the barber cut my hair, all the while hoping with every fiber of my being that my father would come back before the end of the haircut, so that I would not have to suffer the indignity of saying that I had no money. In retrospect, what my father did wasn't unreasonable because I never did tell him how I felt. But having a young impressionable mind made insecure by the lack of money, I felt deeply the humiliation, self-inflicted though it was. Some of the time my father did comeback before the finishing touches, and I would breathe a sigh of relief and promise God that I would be a good boy for answering my prayers. At other times he came back well after the end, and I sat in a waiting chair, mood sullen and eyes slightly red.

I remember one time I came to the barber with my father and older brother Ben. Ben was the brother closest in age to me, and for that reason he was the closest in friendship. I needed a haircut, but I dreaded walking into that shop because regardless of whether he came back on time or not, the wait for my father was excruciating. Thoughts of the wait and the uncertainty weighed heavily, though bravely I tried to put on a strong face because I did not want Ben to notice. He couldn't possibly understand that fear.

As usual, my father nodded to the barber and then escorted me to a chair, my brother in tow. When he instructed the barber to cut my hair short and told me to wait for him to return, I braced myself mentally for the anguish that was to follow. Ben interjected, "Why don't you give Jaime the money, father?"

I was shocked. My young mind whirled as the gears realigned.

"He can pay the barber himself afterwards, father," Ben continued insistently.

I stared at Ben and felt that he knew the feeling of not having money. We were more alike than I had thought, and for a brief moment I saw shades of my childhood fears in his eyes. But his eyes were strong.

That was when I realized I had been sitting in a prison of my own making all along. My sufferings were mostly self-inflicted, and with one simple push Ben demolished the stony Bastille. The walls, impregnable as they seemed, were really made out of Legos. He did not know it, but that day Ben taught me that some problems could be solved by simply asking, and that sometimes the barbed wired fences around our circumstances are of our own making, erected on the assumption that things are the way they should be. Life is hard, but sometime it's harder than it has to be. It's a lesson that I carried into adulthood, though the application of it, in my experience, is easier said than done. Old habits indeed die hard.

When I started high school, my brother Ben left home to join the Navy. One of my few vivid memories of childhood was the moment Ben left for boot camp. I sat on the sofa in the living room. Ben was by the door, standing at the bottom of the stairs, hair neatly cut and a duffel bag in hand. My father stood by Ben. "Take care of yourself, son." His voice broke and trailed off in a quivering note that was on the losing side of self-control. He suppressed a sob and quickly walked up the stairs. Ben stood in place like a pillar of stone, and then turned around and walked out the door. I thought I saw a shimmer in his eyes as he turned around.

It was one of the few times I saw my dad cry.

A few months before my high school graduation, my father asked me to accompany him on a trip to a bank. Like most teenage boys, I had things that I thought I'd rather do than to tag along with my father. "But Dad, I have things to do." His tone, however, was firm, "You have to come, son. It's important."

Once at the bank, my father marched me right up to the cashier. "I'd like to open a savings account for my son, please," he said while beaming. The teller smiled kindly, and my father gingerly fished a wad of cash from his pocket. The edges were slightly tattered, but the bills were clean and neatly bounded with a rubber band widthwise down the center. It was the first time I had seen that much money in one place. I couldn't believe it. "And put this $500 in the account," he added.

So, at seventeen, I had my first checking account. Having never before had more than $100 to my name, I left the bank with $500. That was three years' worth of Christmas, New Year, and birthday money combined. I walked in the bank a young lad, but I walked out a bit taller, my shoulders broader.

Truth be told, I was clueless about money at that point. I had no idea what credit cards were, where to park money long term, how to manage credit scores, what personal withholdings were, or why one should avoid time-share presentations like the plague. I didn't know a premium from a deductible, let alone the differences between liability, collision, and comprehensive coverage. No one had taught me what IRA's and 401(k)s were, or how they were different from one another, or, most importantly, why I should put money away for retirement when I had yet to live my prime. In terms of financial literacy, I was an Amish kid moving to New York City.

In lieu of financial literacy, I had something almost as good—a scarred memory of being poor. My experience in childhood firmly implanted within my sub-consciousness an aversion for having no money. At seventeen, I vividly remembered my 11-year-old self-sitting on a barber chair and wishing to God that the haircut would last longer, just a minute or two longer, so that my father could come back in time. I resolved not to be poor. I didn't know how to acquire or manage money, but I sure as hell knew how *not* to spend it—a life-long habit that straddles the borders of frugality and stinginess, much to the exasperation of my long-suffering wife.

At the age of 18, possessing a car and a checking account with $1,000 but no financial literacy of any kind, I stepped into college. There I remained for many years, oblivious to the coming and passing of the Silver Age.

A JOURNEY OF A THOUSAND MILES

MY FIRST INTRODUCTION TO CREDIT CARD smithing came during the most unremarkable of events: a double-date in a Korean BBQ restaurant.

In the early days of 2012, Delilah and I were planning our wedding. The Silver Age had just ended (though I did not know it at the time), and more than a decade had passed since I left for college. Though graduated from college and holding a job, I had absolutely no idea what airline miles were for, much less what manufactured spending was. I had a single credit card, a Citibank student credit card, opened since the early days of college, which I faithfully used for many years, eschewing all other cards because I wanted to keep my finances simple. The card was a simple 1 percent cashback card, and I remembered feeling a tremendous sense of accomplishment when I was approved for the card on my meager 10-hour-per-week minimum-wage college job—sorting books in the school's medical library. There I was, finally in the big boys club, imbued with a purchasing power that was no longer tied to the balance of my checking account.

It was a great and seductive power. I had a part-time job, a credit card, a girlfriend, but absolutely no idea about financial management, all of which made for a dangerous combination. Luckily, I didn't fall into the downward spiral of credit card debt, thanks to my natural bent for stinginess. I didn't make a lot of money in those poor college days, but I didn't spend much because I was a cheapskate. The scarred memories of my childhood subconsciously manifested themselves in an aversion to debt, though it was an inclination that I had yet to harness productively.

At the time, I had a reasonably good credit score that was in the mid-700s, but I didn't know how much of an asset that score was until Delilah and I had a double date with another couple, Terry and Mary, who were, and still are, true travel aficionados. Terry was a young mild-mannered fellow who hid a sharp observational mind behind his muted exterior, though an occasional hint of his acumen could be seen in the careful and discreet manner in which he observed and took mental notes of everything.

We had our double date at a popular Korean BBQ restaurant, so popular that during opening hours the crowd outside continually threatened to approach Black Friday proportion. They took no reservation, being "first come, first served." Our conversation wandered desultorily before touching on the upcoming wedding. Delilah was in charge of the theme colors and decoration, while my area of responsibility was the honeymoon.

"So, your honeymoon!" Mary clapped her hands excitedly. "Where to?"

"No fixed location. It's a work in progress."

"Oh, you should consider Venice. At that time it is lovely."

"What's so lovely about Venice Beach?" I asked with a frown.

Terry and Mary broke into uncontrolled fit of mirth. "Not Venice Beach, silly. Venice, Italy. You know, Queen of the Adriatic, La Serenissima."

"I was thinking maybe road trip in the United States. Maybe Yellowstone."

"It's your freaking honeymoon. Dream big, man," Terry interjected exasperatedly.

His wife added, "Really, you should go see Venice before it sinks into the Adriatic, and oh, the romance."

"Hmm . . . how about Hawaii?"

"Dream bigger!"

I considered suggesting a cruise ship in Alaska but caught a glance of my wife-to-be, who leaned forward with eyes widened. No man wants to dream small in front of his fiancée.

"What itinerary do you suggest then?"

Mary replied instantly, "Rome, Florence, and Venice. Nothing like living *la dolce vita* and eating gelato every day."

I stole a glance at Delilah and saw her leaning forward even more. "Okay, you got me. Got any discount tips for airfare?"

Mary raised both hands, palms upwards with the tips pointing towards her husband. "Ta-dah! You got the right guy."

Terry used to work for American Airlines as a front-desk ticketing agent, and one of the better perks of his job was the chance to fly American Airlines free in standby. As long as there was an empty seat on an American Airline flight, he and a relative of his choosing could travel free of charge. The way he told it, he made use of the perk often, flying to San Francisco occasionally on Saturday morning to eat oysters along the wharf, enjoy a fancy lunch in Little Italy, and then fly back out in the afternoon, sometime in the business section. His wife told of weekends when he flew over to Tokyo for some sushi and sightseeing and then flew back late Sunday. His plane would dock on the international terminal, and he would leave the plane and walk down a few terminals to start work at his ticketing desk. He had since then left the airline job, but he still managed to travel far and often, though I thought those later travels were mostly feasible because of his work connections.

Our server, Paul, came by to recommend some favorites and gave us some pointers on grilling management. "Really attentive and friendly, isn't he?" Delilah remarked when he left to refill our order. The four of us nodded at one another in agreement. Terry picked up a short rib. "You're lucky because you're going to Europe. You still got seven months, so scoring a free seat is easy."

Feeling like a camera in one of those movie scenes where the camera angles start with a view of the globe and then gradually pan in, going from global to continental, national, regional, and eventually focusing on a particular person or building, I zeroed in on the word *free*.

"Did you say *free* seat?"

"Sure did." He saw my puzzled look and added, "Airline miles. If you each apply for one credit card that should be enough to fund your trip to Europe."

"You mean the banks are going to give me $1,000 worth of airfare for a measly card application?"

"Yes."

"What's the catch?"

He shrugged his shoulders. "How should I know? All I know is I've been doing it for years."

That seemed so egregious a violation of the no-free-lunch rule that if economics were basketball, it'd be considered a flagrant foul. I couldn't quite put my hand on why it worked, but whatever it was, I wanted my hands in it. "Tell me more."

"Nothing comes for free. If you manage to score free flights, you'd better treat us to dinner."

"At this place!" Mary helpfully clarified.

"Sure thing!" Legends have it that Odin sacrificed one of his eyes and hung himself from Yggdrasil nine days and nine nights in exchange for wisdom. I got off lightly with only the price of dinner (though Korean BBQ was slightly on the expensive side). "So what are airline miles?"

"Airline miles are like a sort of currency you can get from applying for credit cards."

"So are they like scrip?"

"Yes. They can be redeemed for flights pretty much anywhere."

"That's straightforward enough. Apply for a card, earn the bonus, book the flight. Is that it?"

Terry had a laugh that reminded me of Antonio Banderas in *The Mask of Zorro* when his student, Zorro, described sword fighting as getting the pointy end into the other guy. Eventually Terry stopped laughing and winked. "It's much more complicated than that. Have you ever read *Fifty Shades of Grey?*"

"Of course not! But I've heard of it."

"The relationship between airlines and frequent flyers is sort of like the one in the book."

"Seriously?"

"Yeah, whips, blindfold, handcuffs and everything."

"So who's the one holding the whip?"

"The airline, of course."

I looked at his face. The needle on my BS detector pointed squarely at zero. "That's not what you said earlier. Free seats, remember?"

"It's a lopsided relationship, but you can switch roles." He lightly flicked his wrist with his chopsticks, "Master the miles, and the airlines will be the ones handcuffed to the bed blindfolded."

Right beside me, Delilah and Mary had already drifted into the more engaging topic of wedding theme colors. Between the hubbub I caught a few words but didn't quite grasp their enthusiasm. I understood money better than I understood women, though to be honest, that's like an English major saying that he understood the theory of general relativity better than he understood quantum mechanics. I leaned forwards towards Terry. "Do tell."

"First thing is that you gotta pick your battlefield. You ever heard of SkyPesos?"

"What's that? A Mexican airline?"

"Ha! That's the name of a major American airline program."

"Why'd they call themselves SkyPesos?"

"They didn't. Travel hackers did." He added, "And that's Argentinean pesos, not Mexican pesos."

"So?"

"So you gotta earn miles smartly. Not all programs are the same, you see. Some are so hard to use they're pretty much worthless."

Terry continued to give me a crash course on the finer points of airline miles. I got no further than the basics, and we tarried half an hour after the grill was shut off, chatting about renewing expiring miles and earning miles through brokerage deposits. Paul continued to stop by to refill our glasses. When it came time to settle the bill Terry paid, using a United Airlines credit card.

Delilah waved Paul over as we stood up. "That was excellent service! You're one of the best waiters we ever had."

He beamed and she pressed on, "Is there a feedback form we can fill for you?"

"Unfortunately, there isn't. But I can get the manager if you want."

The manager came by, and Delilah gushed on the 5-star service. She glanced around the completely-packed restaurant. "Incredibly good food as well. You run the best Korean BBQ place in the whole city."

High praise considering that the city was called Little Seoul, but it was sincere and well deserved. He shook our hands and handed out his business cards. His name was Martin.

"This is our favorite. Well worth the hour-long wait," I added.

"Well, we're friends now, you see," Martin said as his eyes crinkled into a smile. "Next time just ask the host to call me, and you won't have to wait."

<hr>

Terry had given me a good primer on the art, leaving me well equipped to continue my mastery through self-study. Once home, I immediately made a beeline for the computer and did a search on *credit card churning* and *app-o-rama*, and spent the next hour in the study surrounded by virtual displays of credit card offers, bonuses, miles-earning methods, ways to extend miles expiration, redemption choices, point transfers, partner airlines, and hotel programs. If this were a movie, this scene would probably best be captured with a camera rotating around the computer before zooming into my eye, where the viewer could see the slightly warped reflection of the screen in my iris, across which images after images of text and credit cards flickered.

I looked up from the screen, which now glowed palely against the yellow tint of the fluorescent bulbs of the study. The emptiness of the night filled the room with silence except for the tirelessly methodical ticking of the wall clock, which indicated that it was slightly pass eleven o'clock. About two hours had passed. The room seemed a bit smaller as if somehow the world had shrunk while I studied. Or perhaps my dreams just grew bigger. I recalled an advertisement I'd seen earlier on a miles card advertisement. It was an image of a young man hunching over a surfboard, his paddling motion frozen against a gorgeous backdrop of the deep blue ocean while an idyllic mountain stood tall and inviting in the distance. The saturated blue and green hues evoke a primal thirst for the bliss of the ocean and great outdoors, tugging on heartstrings attached to wanderlust that I never knew I had.

Turned out I had a wanderlust after all. It was just buried beneath stinginess all these years.

I leaned back and took a deep breath. Terry was right; the world of airline mileage had a steep learning curve. It wasn't easy or straightforward, but at least those who were willing to put in the hours could expect to be accordingly rewarded.

The next morning, I sat from the table across from my wife. Channeling Neo from *The Matrix* when he comes out of the kung fu upload, I said dramatically, "I know airline miles."

"Uh . . . what?"

"I can get free flights anywhere in the world now."

She stopped her spoon midair. "Anywhere?"

"Anywhere . . . as long as it's within United States and Europe," I admitted. "It's my first time on the snow, so I'd better stick to the beginner slopes."

"I don't mind Hawaii, actually. I saw a cruise that goes around the four islands."

I recalled what little I knew of Hawaii, and the foremost images that come to mind were just beaches and palm trees, which we had in spades in Southern California. As a boy, I loved reading western history, especially the Middle Ages, and literary classics from authors like Dickens, Tolstoy, Cervantes, Austen, Dumas, so Europe felt like a friend I'd yet to meet. Hawaii, on the other hand, I knew nothing about except for what could be gleaned from an episode or two of *Hawaii Five-O*. Lots of violence and constant gun battles, if that show was to be believed. I uttered the words that I would come to regret: "Hawaii seems boring. I don't know what I'd do for two weeks on Hawaii."

She made an executive decision. "We'll do both. But Europe first."

(When we eventually made it to Hawaii, we enjoyed it immensely. There were enough activities to last a month, let alone two weeks. Delilah and I discovered a love for snorkeling, which Hawaii provided amply with utmost pristine quality, ranking among the top few destinations to snorkel in the entire world. My love for Hawaii cost me dearly, though. Ever since I admitted my undying love for the Aloha state, anytime that I dismiss a potential vacation destination as boring or lacking in activities, Delilah would *gleefully* remind me of "boring" Hawaii. I would never live that one down.)

Having received the green light, I applied for two American Airlines credit cards (50,000 miles each) and met the minimum spending requirements within two months. As promised, the miles were deposited shortly thereafter, and I parlayed them into two round-trip tickets to Europe. My wife wanted to see Rome, Florence, and Venice, so I devised an itinerary in which we flew into London and stayed for five nights before making our way to our next home base Vienna, from which we made daytrips to Budapest and Prague. From there we continued onto the Seven Hills of Rome, the Renaissance streets of Florence, and finally the floating canals of La Serenissima.

The transatlantic flights cost only 80,000 American Airline miles, well within the 100,000 miles we acquired through the two applications. I was, and still am, quite proud of the achievement. Not bad for a first outing, if I do say so myself.

FIRST HONEYMOON

WE LOVED OUR THREE-WEEK HONEYMOON IN Europe. We still remember those days fondly, the memories made sweeter by the fact that Citibank footed the airline bill. It was an eye-opening experience to see life outside of the United States. It was also sobering. While cultures and norms are different, the needs of life are the same everywhere. I used to think of Europe as the land of idyllic romance, but look closer and you'd find the same struggle to make a living. The demands of money come to all lives.

Overcast sky greeted us in London after an 11-hour flight on British Airways. It was our first flight on a foreign carrier. Having travelled on a fair number of US domestic flights for work, I found the foreign airlines much more generous in terms of comfort and entertainment. The seats in economy class were actually comfortable, and I couldn't believe the in-flight entertainment was free of charge. It was as if these foreign airlines were somehow immune to the American prime directive of squeezing every single penny possible from passengers. When the stewardess came by offering an in-flight beverage, Delilah inquired after the price of a glass of wine.

"Honey, you're on British Airways," the stewardess snickered. "Wine is free." Apparently, there are sometimes better alternatives to the American way.

Looking outside the window while the airplane taxied to the gates, I could see a light drizzle set against a vast cloud-covered sky. Only a faint reddish region broke the monotony of gray to hint at where the sun was hiding behind the cloud. The clock on my phone indicated that it was only three o'clock in the afternoon, yet it felt like dusk.

The trip from the airport to our hotel near Victoria station added greatly to the fatigue from the transatlantic flight. We each had a backpack and a luggage, and the latter squeaked unhappily as we dragged them over the cobblestone while occasional large drops of water accumulating under foliage pelted our umbrellas. We had a devil of a time finding the hotel because apparently the British, despite being the erstwhile empire on which the sun never set, haven't gotten around to a sensible street labeling system. That's probably why they eventually lost control of the empire, I thought viciously while searching the streets. Delilah eventually enlisted the help of a passerby, and we found our hotel. Shortly thereafter we fell, arms widespread, backwards onto the soft comfort of the bed.

We visited the British National museum, where we viewed the famous Parthenon friezes that I once studied in my college Arts History class. From there we toured the major monuments like Westminster Abbey, London Eye, Big Ben, St. Paul's Cathedral, and the Tower of London, interspersing sightseeing with an occasional museum visit. Remarkably, the museums were mostly free, many of which could stand toe-to-toe with the best of the museum anywhere. Being believers of the adage that half the fun of travel is trying the cuisine, we sampled traditional cuisine such as cockles and whelks (chewy), eel and pie (slimy), bangers and mash (stick-to-your-ribs), fish and chips (tasty), and haggis (surprisingly mild-tasting). We came away with a new appreciation for British history and a better understanding of why there isn't a British restaurant on every corner of America as there are, say, Japanese, Mexican, Italian, or Thai. Portion size, we noted, was much smaller. The British pay more and eat less, but they eat well.

On the second-to-last day In London, we visited Borough Market, which charmingly lay underneath an overhanging freeway. Terry and Mary advised us of a friendly couple of locals manning a goat-milk ice-cream stand in the back of the market, so we dropped by after visiting the nearby Tate Modern. True enough, the stand was there. The offerings were a bit on the pricy side at three pounds for a small (not American small, European small) cup.

We bought a small cup and continued on our way. This goat-milk ice cream was very delicate with floral notes. It had the smooth feel of custard and the richness of gelato tied together by a hint of meadows. Delilah immediately turned around and walked back to the stand. "This is good!" she exclaimed.

The owner, a middle-aged gentleman with overalls, brightened. "Glad you like it. Where in the States are you from?" he said in an accent that brought to mind *Braveheart*.

"Los Angeles. How do you know we're from the States?"

He handed us a sample cup with honey-flavored goat-milk ice cream. "Yankee accent. How long you're visiting London for?"

"Four days and five nights."

He shook his head. "You need a month, at least."

"We'll be back someday. It's only across the pond," I said. Delilah shot me a look, the kind that mockingly said, "Who are you, and what did you do with my husband?"

"Must be great living in London," I said while nibbling on the free sample. "With the arts, culture, history, and everything."

He shrugged. "It has its drawbacks. Grass is greener on the other side, you see." He handed us another sample, this time caramel flavored.

I surveyed the market. "Doesn't seem like there are many tourists here."

"Not many come here. It's just as well."

"Really?"

"Tourists can be fickle. My mum calls them 'cultural rats'." He grinned. "Present company excepted, of course."

"Cultural rats?"

"Ya know. Show up and make a mess of things. You can't get rid of them. First to leave when ship is sinking."

"Your mum sounds like a wacky person."

"Bloody right you are. But she's mum all the same, you know."

Before leaving we purchased another small cup, but he waved off our money. "Enjoy your honeymoon," he said and grinned.

Vienna was only a short two-hour flight away from London. It had a similar feel to London except for the Germanic influences on the cuisine and language (one step forward and one step backward), plus a passion for music. It was early November, and Jack Frost had already established his seasonal retreat in the city. Landing at the airport, Delilah was initially apprehensive, it being her first time in a non-English-spoken country. So was I, though I put on a brave face and said, "Let's just wing it." About two hours and several subways later, we managed to arrive at our hotel none the worse for wear. Turned out the fears were unwarranted; the Austrians were as warm as their weather was cold.

From Vienna, we took a day trip to Prague, where we toured the city starting from the historic Prague Castle and St.

Vitus Cathedral, winding through to Charles Bridges, and eventually ending up downtown in the famous Old Town Square beneath the iconic astronomical clock tower. In Budapest, we found a hole-in-the-wall restaurant with the most delectable kabob plates, which we bought and ate, picnic style, in the grand square in front of St. Stephen's Cathedral. Imagine our surprise when we stumbled across the statue of Ronald Reagan, standing confident in a square (named Freedom Square, I later learned), where a red-brick dome rose in the distance. A familiar face so far from home! I have a picture of Delilah shaking President Reagan's hand, his frozen larger-than-life palm engulfing hers while both smiled broadly.

On the third day, I took off one afternoon for a run around Vienna. The itinerary was simple: a straightforward four-mile run on the Ringstrasse which circumscribed much of Old Vienna and the first district.

About half an hour into the run, a gathering of people on the banks of the Danube piqued my curiosity. On the pavement next to the river, a gentleman of about forty in a leather jacket had constructed a make-shift table. He had a hard face, and his hands smoothly shuffled three foam cups on the table. As he shuffled, he bantered with a swagger that reminded me of the oleaginous dice-game operator I had seen as a child. Underneath one of the cups was a wad of paper shaped into a ball, which the bystanders could occasionally see when the clumsy hands of the operator tilted the wrong cup. "Bet a little, win a little. Bet a lot, win the lot," he bellowed in what sounded like a British accent.

I followed the course of his hands as the three cups swished on the table. The operator seemed extraordinarily inept at the game, shuffling so slowly that anyone with room-temperature IQ could tell which cup the ball was under. He waved a fist clutching a bill in my direction. "Fancy a try? Free five euro bet." I raised my hand upwards with palm facing out and waved it back and forth.

One fellow, however, seemed to be engaged in the game with exaggerated zeal. He wore a baseball cap with the visor backwards and clothes that seemed one size too small. His pants didn't quite come down to his ankle, resulting in a Steve Urkel-like look. He was the only one playing the game. Despite the clumsy shuffling, Short Pants made the wrong guess half the time. On one round, the operator accidentally knocked on the middle cup as the shuffling came to an end, revealing a quick glimpse of the ball inside. Inexplicably, Short Pants betted €10 on the left cup, which he promptly lost.

One young tourist stepped up. Asian, he seemed, and probably in his late twenties or early thirties. He wore a Seattle Mariners jacket with the number 51 emblazoned below the name Ichiro. His companion reached and touched his arm, which he rebuffed with a reassuring pat.

The operator held the euro bill aloft. "Free bet?" Flicking a quick declining wave, Ichiro then slapped down a €20 note. A small shockwave spread through the crowd, and everyone gathered a bit tighter around the table.

The inept shuffling disappeared and the cups whirled round the table in dizzying choreography. I couldn't follow the track of the ball, and judging from the slight murmurs from the crowd, no one else could. The cups eventually came to rest on the table, and the operator withdrew his hands. He looked up with a slight smirk, the kind that telegraphed, "Go ahead, make my day."

Beside me an elderly tourist leaned close to his companion. "This guy's off his rocker," he whispered.

Ichiro stood smiling and uncowed. He stepped closer and leaned down slightly as if to examine the cups better. Everyone tittered as the he started reaching for the cup on the right, but he hesitated and withdrew.

He pointed to the middle cup. "This one."

Before the operator even had a chance to reach down, Ichiro seized the cups on either side, one hand each, and pulled them off the table. There was no ball underneath either cup. Surprised murmurs rose from the crowd. I myself nodded appreciatively at the gambit.

Ichiro stood back and folded his arms. The middle cup, the chosen one, remained upside-down on the table. All eyes focused on the operator, who stood watching with steely eyes.

"POLICE! POLICE!"

A primal shock ran through my body like a jolt of electricity and I involuntarily scanned over my shoulders. Fear that watching the game somehow made me complicit with this con man made hair stood on ends. It quickly passed but the disorder among the crowd did not. In the commotion the operator had grabbed the table, the €20 note included, and hightailed it down the river bank. No police was in sight and definitely none was coming. No one can identify who raised the alarm, though I remember that the voice sounded suspiciously similar to that of Short Pants. He also disappeared in the commotion.

Ichiro stood thunderstruck. His companion whispered something in his ear and he shrugged. Together they disappeared into the crowd, and I continued with my jog.

Rome came as a shock after the relative order of London and Vienna. Traffic was chaos personified: the Italians apparently have a discretionary view for rules and schedule.

Back in Vienna, the locals deemed it inconceivable to jaywalk even when no cars are within sight, and one could set a watch on the trains' arrivals. Here in Rome, the traffic and bus system treat order and timetables like mere moral suggestions. It is said that Mussolini managed to make the trains run on time, though a quick look at Rome indicated that punctuality seemed to have left along with the dictatorship. The haphazard street traffic, in particular the blasé jaywalking, bewildered us initially, but we acclimated in short order. When in Rome, do as Romans do.

By the time we arrived at the City of Seven Hills, we had discovered a secret: All major European cities are bipolar. There is the day side, characterized by, among other things, tourists crowding over attractions, young couples and groups taking photos using selfie sticks, children running amok, scam artists and pickpockets plying their trades, and photographers playing with camera angles and lightning. At night, however, the cities take on a completely different atmosphere—more serene and subdued. Night lights illuminated buildings and moments in a soft hue that freed photographers from the tyranny of intractable clouds. Tourists retreated to their lodgings, as did scammers and pickpockets. The cacophony of the city slowed down to a murmur. If the day side was a flowing stream singing the song of changes, then the night side was a quiet pond purring of serenity.

The transition between the two faces was what photographers called the golden hour. We caught this once in St. Peter's Square. Having visited Vatican museum and the Sistine chapel in the morning, we queued outside St. Peter's square for admittance to the basilica. The line stretched for half the circumference of the square snaking between the enormous colonnades. Delilah poked me. "Look that way," she said, pointing in the direction of the Egyptian obelisk in the center. The sun was setting behind the white dome of the Vatican. In the dying moments of the day, it breathed orange-red life into the billowing clouds, its lingering rays lighting haloes on the statues of saints and disciples lining the colonnades' roof.

We thought the better of it, left the queue, and sat on the pavement observing the twilight. "Beautiful, isn't it?" Delilah asked while leaning close. Together we watched dying orange flares as the sun went blazing into the good night.

Our last night in Rome, we walked from our hotel to the top of the Spanish Steps, where local artists gathered and sketched portraits for tourists. From the high vantage point, one could see numerous dark figures sitting on the countless stair steps that cascaded downwards, curving around a viewing platform and eventually flowing to a small, lighted fountain at the bottom. Making our way down the steps, we eventually rambled to Trevi Fountain. By that hour of night, the fountain had metamorphosed into an oasis of tranquility. We found a seat on the right banks of the fountain, where we huddled against the cold and watched the world flow by.

The crowd thinned as the night deepened. Occasionally, some walked into the fountain from a connecting alley and tarried a while before exiting, their lives and ours touching briefly for the space of a few minutes at the fountain. Some tossed coins into the fountain, a tradition that according to legend would ensure a return to Rome. The lonely melody of a street musician echoed from a distant alley. Flowing waters danced from the ageless marble carvings, as it have in centuries past when we were yet born, and as it will in century to come when we are long gone. In that moment, we caught a glimpse into the Italian ethos of *la dolce vita*—the sweet life.

The further north we went in Italy, the more orderly traffic seemed. Florence was largely immune to the controlled chaos plaguing the street of Rome. On the morning of the second day, we visited the church San Miniato al Monte. It sat high above the city at the top of a long flight of stairs that extended from a bus stop through a pair of metal gates and eventually culminated at a plateau in front of the Basilica's door. The view of the Arno River and the Ponte Vecchio (the Old Bridge) stretched below like a gigantic still-life painting. From that high vantage point, the city stood serene and unchanging, the occasional movement being the shimmering water of the Arno, the scurrying of the ant-sized cars, and the lazy drift of the clouds.

We sat perched on the parapet watching the city below. Foot traffic on the winding stairs flowed constantly in either direction. About halfway down the stairs (immediately outside the metal gates), a man and a woman had set up a white plastic table plying the old sign-and-donate scam. They stood pen in one hand and clip board in the other. The choice of location was not accidental, nor was their choice of official-looking uniforms. For the unaware both telegraphed the impression that their petition had the imprimatur of the church. Earlier when we passed by, they had held out a clipboard to Delilah. On the clipboard was a petition written in Italian. "Can you sign against the drugs?" one asked. We waved it off, not because we were for drugs, but because we knew their modus operandi.

Among the throng they managed to ensnare an elderly couple, Midwestern American tourists, if my first impression was any judge. The lady had scribbled a quick signature, and these two scammers were vociferously demanding a donation. One held up the signed petition and tapped impatiently at the bottom. If the *scam* section of my guidebook was correct, the message he was pointing to was "Minimum €20 donation required."

The lady attempted to reason in vain. One scammer, a college-aged clean-shaven fellow with hair neatly combed, practically hollered at the couple continuously in Italian. Passersby stopped and became onlookers. Under the pressure of abuse and indifferent peering eyes, the lady capitulated. She fished out a bill and disgustedly plopped it on the table.

Tension deflated and onlookers continued on their way. The scammers pocketed the bill. One held out the clipboard to the lady's husband and raised the pen invitingly with the other hand. The husband declined.

Watching as the scam transpired, I had a light bulb moment. All things can be exchanged for money, including intangible traits such as honesty and integrity, or even a clean conscience! I already knew of the basics: the day laborer trades in his sweat, the doctor his knowledge, the craftsman his skills, and the artist his creativity. But even character traits or fundamental rights have value. Criminals, for instance, risk the loss of freedom when holding up a bank. A mere fifty yards or so below me, these two scammers were trading clean consciences for "donations." Every day on television reality stars trade in their dignity and privacy for 15 minutes of fame. In certain parts of Nevada, one could find a good market for love and intimacy, or at least lease them for a while. In Washington DC, integrity and honesty could be bought and sold for profits that those peddling their freedom or conscience could only dream of.

Airline miles came to mind, and I thought about the trip to Europe. Subtracting taxes and fees, we saved over $2,000 on airfare. What quality or trait did I use to save so much money? It wasn't time or sweat—the card applications and bookings took no more than five hours. It didn't cost me a dirty hand neither, my conscience stood entirely clean.

All lives strive. Some thrive, but hard is the lot for most. Why was it that these two grafters ply their trade at the cost of their conscience but likely make less than I did in five hours with credit cards? Someone ought to be paying for all these discounts, rewards, and benefits. I wondered who.

For the final destination of the honeymoon we left the autumn drizzles in Florence and took the train to Venice. The Italian sun was in full attendance, shining on the city with photogenic luminance while not being oppressively hot. Our hotel was not located far from the train station, but we had a devil of a time finding it because the Venetians, like the British, found no use in a practical street-marking system. Imagine the labeling system of the British, but throw in Italian efficiency and you got the maze that was Venice. Along the way we passed by gangways—wide wooden planks that stood about two feet above the ground on metal support. They ran along the length of major thoroughfares though we knew not their functions.

Curiously, the hotel receptionist, a pretty girl in her late twenties who spoke five languages, offered us a choice of an upstairs or ground-level room. Fancying myself wise in the ways of Europe, I inquired whether the hotel had an elevator. Hearing responses to the negative, we opted for the ground-level room. The receptionist had a sympathetic look that reminded me of Monty Hall's when his contestants chose the door with the goats.

The room itself was pretty, sensibly decorated with flower pots on the windowsill and a side window looking into a small garden. A lingering smell of dampness reminded me of wet clothes and waterlogged carpets. A milieu of mildew hovered in the air. Some conversation with another tourist revealed the cause. A day or two earlier there had been an *acqua alta*, a seasonal high-water event when the tide rose as high as three feet above normal level and inundated most of the ground in Venice, though the effects are rather inconvenient than crippling. When my wife and I were walking about Florence in the summer Italian rain, most of Venice was under a few inches of water. The wooden gangway in the main streets apparently served as an elevated walkway on which locals and tourists alike could travel without getting wet. We attempted a room change, but the window of opportunity had closed. Hoping for the best, we stashed personal belongings and luggage a few feet off the ground and ventured forth into the city.

That night we took a ride on a *vaporetto* (that's what they called the water bus) down the Grand Canal. Delilah and I secured a spot near the starboard railing, where I stood with my hands wrapped around her shoulder watching Venice float by. The lights illuminating the city bounced off the rippling surface of the canal to produce waving sinuous reflections on the water. Braced against the wind and looking at the many buildings that lined the canals, many of which were unlit in the dark, we felt keenly the elegant decline of this once-powerful city. This was the former Queen of the Adriatic, she of maritime fame who sacked Constantinople—the capitol of the eastern Roman empire—and eventually brought the Byzantine empire to its knees. Buildings that in centuries past bustled with life and wealth now stood forlorn and abandoned. Unlit edifices, their occupants long fled, traced lonely silhouettes in the night, bearing witness to the vicissitudes of Time and Fortune.

In St. Mark's square we sat down on one of the wooden gangways that remained from the *acqua alta* and basked in the romance-drenched atmosphere of La Serenissima. The cafés facing the square had their orchestras out in full force, serenading an adoring crowd. To be honest, anyone could see that these four-man musical ensembles were orchestras in the same manner that a go-cart is a car. But Love is blind, they say. To the left of our gangway seat was a café where four musicians in full tuxedos played an upbeat tune. In the middle of the square, two or three couples waltzed to the music while several gypsies walked the square, peddling propeller-like fluorescent toys. Occasionally, one of them shot the toy high into the night air with the aid of an elastic band. Zipping skywards, the propellers fluttered down slowly, their twirling blades tracing out blue arcs against the deep darkness of the sky.

On the vaporetto ride home, we stood on the deck near the railings. A portly man in overalls boarded the boat at the Palazzo Cavalli stop. He pushed a large dolly on which three boxes were stacked up taller than my head. Deftly maneuvering the dolly between the dock and the boat, he wheeled it next to us and gave a salutary nod. He seemed to be in his early 60s. The rocking of the boat seemed no inconvenience to him and his wheeled charge.

After the boat lurched into the shimmering canal, a ticket inspector emerged from the hold of the boat. He wore a dark-blue uniform and seemed no more than 25. With vacant eyes he approached the passengers, inquiring of each, *"Biglietto?"* We flashed our fare stubs and he moved on.

Our neighbor waved a plastic card to the inspector, who stared at the dolly fixedly. Awakening from the robotic routine, he gestured at it spiritedly. We stood not understanding a single word, but inferred that the dolly was either not allowed or lacking permit. Ashen-faced, our neighbor made a feeble protest. He pointed down the canal and put two hands, palms vertical and facing each other, about six inches apart. Just a little bit, he seemed to say.

Two or three locals interjected on behalf of the porter. An elderly Italian lady covered in shawls scolded and gesticulated angrily at the inspector, who stood with stony resolve. Eventually he barked a few words authoritatively and ended the discussion. Our neighbor sighed and removed his wallet. Face taut, he counted out a few bills, for which the inspector wrote a ticket and a receipt. He perfunctorily checked the rest of the deck and returned to the hold.

Our neighbors stood in place. I stole a glance in his direction and saw a spirit deflated. He stood, shoulders slumped, gazing into the forlorn sky. His large calloused hands gripped the railings tautly, and the reflection of the dancing water falling on his face seemed to lose their mirth. At the next stop he wheeled the dolly around and disappeared into the night.

Delilah stood staring into the water with pensive eyes. I knew she was thinking of her father, who also worked as a porter. Even though past retirement age, he still drove a truck to haul away rubbish and moved sofas and beds. "Life is hard everywhere, isn't it?" she mused.

I thought of my childhood and squeezed her hand. "Sometimes harder than it has to be."

TRAPPED IN MINIMUM SPENDING

FOLLOWING THE HONEYMOON, MY HEART FIRMLY belonged to Europe. For days afterwards, I pored over the pictures of the trip wondering where the time went. I even went online and gazed longingly at grainy live-camera feeds of St. Mark Square, wishing that time could rewind so I'd be back in the Old Continent.

Reflecting on the photos one night, I had yet another light bulb moment. Life is really just made up of memories. Thoughts, values, prejudice, and biases are but products of what we remember, filtered through the lenses of mood and temperament. These cumulative life experiences, whether remembered, deep-seated, or forgotten, make up who we are and what we do. We are given but three score and ten years, and at the end what shall we have but memories of bygone days. But the thing about memories is that they are not egalitarian. Days spent punching the clocks and going through the motions are forever lost in the midst of time, or at best retrieved in indistinct slippery wisps. Such is the lot of life. But when one celebrates and makes merry the memories burn bright. Looking back at the previous year, months and days seem to meld into a collection of formless memories with gaping lacuna. When I thought about the honeymoon, however, scenes of laughter, getting lost, food, making friends, and nighttime monuments jumped out in sharp relief against the fog of time.

I shared the epiphany with the wife. She thought it over a bit. "You forgot relationships."

"What, like love?"

"No, like kinship, friendship, and love."

"Those are included in memories!"

"But you got them backwards. Life is made of relationships, not memories."

I shook my head. "I think *you* got them backwards."

"How are you supposed to celebrate and make merry without family, friends, or loved ones?"

I conceded the point. When she's right, she's right. "But you got a point about travel, though," she added.

"Which point?"

"About seeing the world. I'm so glad we were able to see Europe while we still have the energy."

That reminded me of an observation about Time, Energy, and Money, of which a person can only possess two at each stage in life. We had Time and Energy, and Chase was providing the Money. Might as well.

I sat up straight. "I have a proposition for you."

"Shoot."

"I know we planned otherwise, but let's postpone kids for a year or two. "

Her eyes brightened. "Oh?"

I nodded. "Let's do another honeymoon in Europe."

"But we already had a honeymoon."

"You're such an awesome wife that a single honeymoon isn't enough."

She gave my arm a rap. "You're such a smooth talker."

I winked. "I might have nothing going for me, but I'm honest." Remembering the card applications, I added, "But I'll need to borrow your identity."

"Take my social security number. You got me at 'honeymoon'."

Agreement in place, I started applying for credit cards every three months or so. Stockpiling airline miles was the primary emphasis. I eventually developed a workflow and a spreadsheet to track the progress of credit card applications. Meticulous recordings of sign-up vitals (sign-up dates, security words, minimum spending required, and dates to call for cancellation) kept the entire process manageable, though not entirely painless.

In late 2013, Citibank offered an Executive Platinum card with 100,000 American Airline miles bonus and a minimum spending requirement of $10,000 within three months. The annual fee was $450 (not waived for the first year) with a statement credit of $200, though the fees were somewhat compensated with free access to American Airlines airport lounges. At an estimate of one cent per mile, that worked out to be $750 rewards per application, so I pulled the trigger and got one under my name. Briefly I considered getting another for Delilah, but dismissed the thought summarily. I couldn't possibly meet $20,000 spending within three months.

The $10,000 minimum spending, I thought, could be met with a mix of Amazon Payment plus personal spending. Terry had earlier put me onto Amazon Payment, a subsidiary of Amazon that processed online transactions. It allowed an account holder to send money to a merchant or, more likely, to his spouse free of charge, with a credit card as the funding source. The spouse could then withdraw to a bank and send money right back using a different credit card as the funding source. The sending and receiving limit for each account was $1,000 per month, but that was more than enough to make it a beloved if not favorite gadget in the travel hacker toolbox.

My wife and I had two Amazon Payment accounts between us, so we could send $6,000 within three months, leaving only $4,000 to be spent on personal expenses. Nothing more than a walk in the park.

A package arrived two days later via first-class mail. The word *Urgent* stood boldly in the front. Inside was a sleek fancy box, the kind that jewelry and diamond retailers use to package necklaces or engagement rings. Holding it aloft, I tried to recall if Delilah had purchased jewelry online recently. The heft of the box was slightly different, if my one experience with the engagement ring store was any judge. This one felt safer. It didn't have the same burning feeling in the hands (and the wallet) as the engagement ring box did.

Throwing the box open, I found the Citibank card. Everything inside the packaging, including the Terms and Conditions booklet, was first class. Who knew that paying a $450 annual fee meant getting pampered like an aristocrat? The royal treatment stood in stark contrast with the typical no-annual-fee mileage cards (of which I had many) that came unceremoniously in nondescript standard-sized envelope.

I activated the card and set up online payment. Pulling out my spreadsheet of card vitals to update the fields under the Executive Platinum card, I noticed that another card, Chase United MileagePlus Explorer, was close to 10 months into its lifetime. Ever since it had accrued me 50,000 miles, the card had been lying in the sock drawer awaiting cancellation. It had an annual fee of $95 (waived for the first year), and I wouldn't want it to be active in two months when the one-year anniversary rolled around.

Time to release the card from its surly bonds. Dialing the numbers on the back, I asked to cancel and was quickly escalated to a retention specialist. Elaine came on the line with a honeyed velvet voice.

"Thanks for being a card customer, Mr. Doughsmith. I hear that you wanted to cancel your card?"

"Yes, that's right."

"May I know the reason for cancellation?"

"I have too many credit cards. Just trying to get my finances in order." A favorite response, it was my credit card version of "it's not you it's me."

"I can waive the annual fee of $95 for the next year. Would that be of interest to you?"

"Thanks . . . but I still want to cancel."

"How about we waive the annual fee and give you 500 miles per month for the next 16 months?"

"Are those miles free?"

"Yes, but you'd have to spend a minimum of $500 per month."

I ran the numbers. That amounted to 8,000 miles, but it wasn't worth the trouble of using the card every month. "That's a tempting offer . . . but I still want to cancel."

"In that case, how about a statement credit of $50 in addition to waiving the annual fee?"

Now we're talking. Fifty dollars for 15 minutes of work was quite respectable. I didn't personally know anyone who earned that rate, and the last time I saw someone who did, she was standing behind the window in Amsterdam's Red Light District wearing lingerie. But maybe, just maybe . . . Elaine hadn't used her best card yet. "That's a very tempting offer, Elaine." A slight practiced pause. "But . . . can you cancel it anyway?"

"I can offer 15,000 United miles if you spend $3,000 within the next three months." Score! "The annual fee, however, won't be waived," she added.

I could have negotiated the annual fee, but thought it best not to push further. I could cancel one month into the second year and get the annual fee refunded. "You've been very persuasive, Elaine. I'll take the offer." I hung up and did a fist pump. A free 15,000 miles without having to apply for a new card was nothing to sneeze at. Earned a short reprieve, the Chase United had.

It then dawned on me. A further $3,000 had been added to my commitment. I breathed out a long nervous breath. It was still technically doable, but only in the sense that running a half-marathon was doable for someone who ran five miles a week.

The gods of airline bonuses were relentless in their favor. A few days later, an email from US Airways arrived in my email account. "Earn 15,000 bonus miles with your card," it read. "To qualify, spend $750 each month for the next three months." That email was linked to my US Airways Dividend Miles card, which had already earned 40,000 miles and was lying in the sock drawer awaiting its time to join the choir invisible.

I had a suspicion that my wife's US Airways card also received the same offer. The gods do love toying with us for sport. Sure enough, hers did.

According to my calculations $750 per month for three months was $2,250. Between the four offers, I had to spend $17,500 within three months! What started out as a walk in the park was now the Boston marathon. My mood was deflated like a football after a New England Patriot game. No way was I going to make it.

A week later, I shared my story of the perfect minimum-spending storm over dinner with my sister. She listened bemusedly and shook her head. "First world problem!"

"You're supposed to sympathize with your poor brother, you know."

"It is what it is," she mused. "You two are so alike."

"Who?"

"You and Harry."

"He's into miles too?" I puzzled.

"No, but he has like twenty credit cards." She waved a finger at herself. "He even borrowed my name for applications."

"What kind of applications?"

"I dunno." She raised her brow. "Wait a minute, you should call him."

"Why?"

"He spends like a ton of money every month on cards. You should see his garage."

"What does that have to do with anything?"

"He has a three-gallon plastic container full with gift cards. That thing weighs a ton."

Harry was my older brother, four years older than Ben and eight years my senior. Financially savvy, he was easily the most gifted in the family. From our humble 10-person, two-bedroom apartment beginning, my sister and I took the express train to the middle class by going to college. My brother Ben went by the scenic bus, going first into the Navy and then completing college on the GI bill. But Harry had jogged most of the way. At 19 with only one year of community college, he went to work trying his hands at numerous jobs like computer technician, newspaper delivery, and day trader. Eventually he settled down with a small retail business. In his hands, his modest income multiplied like the five loaves and two fish at

Bethsaida. He eventually entered the real estate business and now owns several houses that he rents. His climb up the economic ladder was the steepest, but also the quickest. By the age of 35 he was semi-retired by choice.

The gap of eight years seemed like an unbridgeable gulf when I was growing up. I'd left home at 18, so we didn't talk often, and even when we did, there wasn't much to talk about. I dialed him up and went straight to topic. "I applied for a few credit cards and now I have a big problem."

"But why're you calling me?"

"Because Fiona said you're expert at credit cards."

Harry was slightly amused. "True that. What's your problem?"

"I need to spend 17k within three months."

"Only 17k?"

"Yes."

"I thought you said you had a problem."

"That's the annual income at minimum wage! In three months!"

"Okay, fine. Have you heard of Amazon Payment?"

"Already have two accounts."

"Hmm . . . you're a bit late on the Costco boat."

"What's the Costco boat?"

"Buy with credit card and return for cash. Too bad it's gone." His voice rang with merriment. "You could've bought four engagement rings and called it a day."

He paused for a moment. "Have you heard of Kiva loans?"

"The one where you make loans to low-income businesses in poor countries?"

"Yup, you can fund the loans with a credit card." He added mischievously, "You can be one part Gandhi and one part Jesse James."

"Er . . . what?"

"You know, be the change you want to see in the world while making out like a bandit."

I recalled what I knew of Kiva, which wasn't much. They did good deeds in the world. That much I knew. I could get onboard with that. "Tell me more."

"Basically you lend out money for six months to a year . . ."

"A whole year?" I gasped.

"What, too long for you?"

"I can't float 10k for the whole year."

"Okay, then I shouldn't tell you that you might lose money on Kiva."

That clinched it. "I guess I'm more Jesse James than Gandhi. What else you got?"

"Well, there's always the good old EvolveMoney. It's a website that lets you pay bills using debit cards. Tell me the name of your mortgage lender."

After I told him, he went silent for a bit, and the sound of typing echoed faintly in the background. "You're out of luck," he declared. "Your mortgage lender isn't on the payee list."

Seemed like it just wasn't my day.

Harry said, "I got another idea. You like running, right?"

"Uh, yes?"

"You can sign up for charity races and ask for donations from friends. Collect donations in cash; pay the organizer with credit card. *Voila.*"

"That's crazy! Do you know how many marathons I'd have to run to collect 17k?"

"Yeah, it's pretty crazy," he conceded.

"Got anything else?"

Harry thought for a while. "You got two options."

"Okay?"

"One, make me an authorized user, and I'll do the spending for you. Just reimburse me the gift card fees."

I was intrigued. "And number two?"

"I'll teach you to do it yourself, but I'm not responsible if you shoot yourself in the foot."

You know what they say: Give a man a fish; he'd eat for a day. Teach a man to fish, and he might compete in the White Marlin Open someday. Scrambling to grab a pen, I perched myself on the dining chair. "I'll take my chances. Give me door number two."

"Alright, so the idea is to buy gift cards with credit cards. Then take the gift cards and pay off your credit cards."

The mechanics of this game snapped together like a jigsaw puzzle with magnetic pieces. That explained the three-gallon tub of gift cards in his garage.

"So where do you get these gift cards?"

"Oh, that's easy. Grocery stores like Ralphs, Wal-Marts, Vons, Albertsons, and Stater Brothers. Drug stores like CVS, Walgreens, and RiteAid have them too." As I hastened to scribble down the names, he added, "But don't buy gift cards at Wal-Mart."

"Why is that?"

"Because Wal-Mart is where you liquidate gift cards. Don't crap where you eat."

I wrote *Don't crap at Wal-Mart.* "So, how do I liquidate?"

"Ah, now we're talking. Got your pencil ready?"

"Yup."

He spent the next 20 minutes giving me a run-down on the basics. "The most important thing is the name," he said at wrap-up.

"What is it?"

"Manufactured spending."

"Weird name." I mentally turned the name around a few time, "But it kind of make sense."

The generation gap seemed smaller when I hung up. A bridge of cards had spanned the divide, and on that bridge I met myself in my brother.

ROOKIE MISTAKES

MY BROTHER WAS RIGHT: ALL THE magic was in the name. Once I knew what manufactured spending was called, I knew where to go on the Internet for further self-study.

If this were a movie—say, *The Wolf of Wal-Mart*—the rest of that week would be a montage of scenes centered on me in a control room, rifling through *Adjustment Bureau*-style holograms. Maybe the camera zooms in on a floating semi-transparent screen prominently featuring the words *Manufactured Spending*. A tap on the screen and an array of secondary holograms cascades upwards to form neat rows on either side. In one, I'd be making a pinching motion to zoom in on a holograph, while in another a swipe of the hand dismisses a screen. In yet another scene I'd be standing frozen gazing at the holograms while another researcher moves in a blur about the room on quadruple speed.

Yep, that's a pretty good description, except let's replace the *Adjustment Bureau* control center with my bedroom, the holographic interface with my computer, the other researcher with my wife, and the archive database with FlyerTalk.

The web site, flyertalk.com, is probably the world's densest repository of frequent flyer and loyalty program knowledge. Founded in 1998 as an online forum for frequent flyer enthusiasts, it has grown into an enormous knowledge base of travel hacking over the years. I found the Manufactured Spending section hidden in a small corner of FlyerTalk. There a fuller picture of the landscape emerged. Every detail of the art of refining profit from credit cards was there: app-o-rama, churning limits, Amex Sync offers, guide for tripling Amex credit line, best available card offers master thread, etc. The learning curve was steep. Like everywhere else on FlyerTalk, the manufactured spending page was riddled with shorthand like CL (credit line), CA (cash advance), AGC (Amex gift cards), AU (authorized user), BB (Bluebird), HP (hard pull), AA (Adverse Action), and FR (financial review), in addition to deliberately obfuscating jargon like Kate (Wal-Mart MoneyCenter Kiosk), beans (Vanilla Reloads), Wally (Wal-Mart), and -4 (7-Eleven).

Bit by bit, the liquidation routes for debit gift cards became clearer. There were three main routes: prepaid reload, credit card bill pay, and money orders. Wal-Mart was the Rome of manufactured spending. Even though other retailers separately offer one or two of those services, Wal-Mart is the only retailer that offers all three. Moreover, it is the only place where one could split a transaction, say a $2,000 money order or a $2,000 bill pay, into multiple payments of $500 each. While that feature doesn't seem to be particularly useful for normal customers, it is the best thing since sliced bread for card smiths because the standard variable-load gift card can carry a maximum of only $500. No wonder this current age is called the Age of Wal-Mart.

By the time Saturday rolled around, I had plotted of locations for all nearby Wal-Marts, Albertsons, Vons, Rite Aid, CVS, Walgreens, Ralphs, and Stater Brothers. The mission was twofold: find the stores that allow gift card purchase on credit, and locate those that sell money orders on debit. It was more of reconnoitering trip. As Machiavelli wrote, "one must learn the nature of the terrain, and know how mountains slope, how valleys open, how plains lie, and understand the nature of rivers and swamps."

It was early in the morning. I glanced outside the car and saw dark clouds billowing low near the horizon. The sun, still swinging on the upward arc, lay completely obscured behind the opaque dark clouds. Its rays, however, lit up the edges of the clouds like burning fringes on a black piece of paper. The day was different. Everything stood out in sharper detail.

First up was Vons.

As I walked to the entrance, I briefly wondered if it would be difficult to find the gift cards. The automated sliding door opened courteously and stepping through I realized I shouldn't have worried. Gift cards were everywhere. In the front of the store was a mini-rack containing prepaid cards and phone reload cards, and in the space between the registers and the aisle were two racks, one free-standing and one attached to an aisle, containing a rainbow assortment of specialty and general cards. Next to the register stood mini-shelves on which gift cards, along with other impulse items, had one more chance to tempt customers. If you were to look closely at any one of the gift cards, however, and you'd see that none of them held value. They all were empty shells of plastic until bought and paid for.

I found my quarry in the Use Everywhere section. Reaching above the $200, $100, and $50 fixed-denomination cards, I gingerly plucked one labeled *Variable load*. The top left corner announced: "Any Amount $20-$500 plus $5.95 Activation Fees" while the bottom left displayed the promise: "Use it anywhere debit cards are accepted."

The cash register area was deserted in the early hours of the morning. An attractive cashier with flowing curly hair stood off to the side of the register, sorting the miscellaneous items on the last-minute impulse racks. My eyes caught hers, and she gestured towards the nearby register. "Be right there," she said. Her name tag said Mindy.

As I shuffled into position across the register, a deep sense of foreboding hovered on the edge of consciousness. Dark scenarios flitted across my minds. Despite the air-conditioned in-store climate, my forehead started to perspire. I slid over the gift card. "Four h-hundred dollars. . . ." I tugged at my collar a bit and added, "Please."

Mindy casually nodded and peeled the back of the card to expose the bar code. She worked slowly and methodically. Judging from the burning sensation in my ears, they must have been bright red. I gazed fixedly at the screen, trying to avoid meeting Mindy's eyes. I wondered if she could see the bright red warning signs that were my ears.

She scanned the barcode, her hands flying over the keyboard in practiced economy. "Four-oh-five ninety-five," she confirmed. The gift card type, last four barcode digits, and the balance due appeared on the checkout screen. She nodded at me. I continued to gaze at the screen intently.

A few seconds passed uncomfortably.

Realization dawned that the ball was in my court. I fumbled in my wallet and took out the American Airlines credit card. Before I swiped the card, however, Mindy turned the gift card over in her hand and furrowed her eyebrow. "Are you going to a graduation party?" she asked.

I thought it a strange question, considering that it was March. I briefly wondered if it was a delaying tactic while she secretly summoned security. Movies always show bank tellers having a secret alarm button, and maybe cashiers have one too. I fumbled for a safe answer. "No. . . . going to a, umm, birthday party." My eyes involuntarily glanced upwards above

Mindy to see if there was a security camera in the corner. If it was possible to sweat bullets, then I was perspiring Magnum-sized rounds.

Mindy turned the gift card packaging around so that the front was facing me. Images of a graduation cap festooned in rainbow confetti decorated the gift card. One corner prominently displayed the words *Happy Graduation.*

"Do you want to get a card that says *Happy Birthday*, then?"

Despite the semi-crippling anxiety attack, I chucked. I couldn't believe I didn't even check the front of the packaging before purchase. What a rookie mistake! Returning to the rack, I picked a Happy Birthday gift card and thanked Mindy for her thoughtfulness.

She repeated the check out procedure to my considerably calmed nerves. After a swipe, the screen flashed *Waiting for Authorization*, and I held my breath for a couple of seconds as the machine ploddingly requested authorization from the great paymaster in the cloud. Without ceremony, it switched into a signature panel. Smiling kindly, Mindy folded the receipt around the gift card lengthwise and handed it over.

That was it. There was nothing to fear; it was just the mind that made it so.

Seeing a customer service counter a few steps away from the cash register, I walked over and tapped on the call bell. A sweet matronly service representative poked her head out from the flower department and said, "Coming right over." Soon she stood behind the counter, her apron still bearing the imprints where she toweled off her hands. "How can I help you?"

Emboldened, I flashed a smile, "Can I get a money order?"

She pulled out a thick folder bearing the logo of Western Union. "How much, honey?"

"Um . . . three hundred dollars?"

Opening the folder, she started riffling through the pages. Half way through, she looked up. "How are you paying?"

I waived my bankcard tentatively, "With a debit card?"

"Sorry dear, cash only."

I put the bankcard back in the wallet and tapped it ruefully. "Never mind. I don't carry that much cash."

"Corporate policy," she said shrugging her shoulders. "Lots of scams going on."

A few miles down the road, I scored a double at a Rite Aid store. The gift card issuer was different here as was the activation fee and, as I quickly came to learn, so were the methods by which the default PIN was set. Debbie was on duty. She was grandmotherly with frazzled white hair, though it seemed that her vivacity hadn't gotten the memo to act age-appropriate. She was one of the rare people who lived the principle that growing old was inevitable, but feeling old was optional.

This time I made sure to choose a gift card with a generic *Congratulations* message. She scanned my $500 gift card matter-of-factly as if I were buying a stick of gum, and soon handed me a receipt for the transaction. I scanned for a place to buy money order and found none. "Where's your customer service counter?" I asked.

"The counter's wherever I am, darling."

"How much is a money order?"

"Let me see . . . 70 cents, I think."

"Can I get one for $399.30?"

Debbie nonchalantly performed her magic at the register. Within thirty seconds, the balance due of $400 appeared on the check-out screen. I drew a sharp breath. Striking gold on my second try, who knew? The card smithing gods must had been in a good mood.

I removed the $400 gift card I had purchased earlier and discreetly peeked at the card number. If the online documentations were correct, the last four of the 16-digit card number were the default PIN. My chest constricting slightly, I swiped the card and entered the PIN.

A small eon seemed to come and pass within two seconds.

The screen displayed *Approved* and the anxiety constricting my chest disappeared like a fog in the morning sun. She handed over the money order. The *To* and *From* fields were blank, but the *Amount* field prominently displayed $399.30.

Immediately next door to Rite Aid was a Bank of America, so I borrowed a pen from Debbie, bless the woman, and scribbled my name under the *From* field. Next to the *To*, I wrote Delilah Doughsmith and in the ATM it went. An auspicious beginning, I thought. Within the space of 40 minutes, my credit card debt had gone up by $405.95, but the money had just packed its belonging and moved across town into my bank account for a few days' holiday.

The rest of the day I continued the survey of grocery stores and drug stores, and by the end of the week I had the lay of the land down. Vons, Albertsons, and Pavillions had no problem with credit cards, but transactions above $500 required a manager override. It is never, ever, a good idea to trigger a manager override. The fewer eyes, the better, and it was far safer to request $495 per card and do multiple transactions if need be. On the other hand, CVS was happy to accept plastic for gift cards, subject to a rolling 24-hour limit of $5,000 per person and enforced by a mandatory swipe of the customer's driver's license. I preferred the latter venue. Under that driver's license policy, cashiers were happy to sell $2,000 or $4,000 a pop without even batting an eye.

Rite Aid was more of a hit-and-miss. Some locations, like Debbie's, had no qualm about accepting credit, but others were more skittish than a deer during open season. Some cashiers claimed that there was a company-wide cash-only policy to deter money laundering. However, even at the same store, enforcement was uneven; some cashiers were sticklers on the rule, while others were completely oblivious. On the other hand, Ralphs had no problem with plastic. They quickly became my favorite stores for obtaining gift cards because there was, at the time, no official limit on purchase amount. Between my wife and me, we could easily get $4,000 per trip per store. Occasionally Ralphs even encouraged it with a promotional $5 in-store coupon for $100 or more in gift card purchases. Oh how we loved those promotions! You know the movie scenes where a couple, having in one way or another acquired a large amount of cash, frolic in their room, throwing dollar bills about with abandon? Same thing with the Ralphs promotion.

It was, unfortunately, much harder to find stores that accepted gift cards for money order purchases. My entire neighborhood only produced two stores that allowed it, though the scarcity was moot due to the ease of obtaining them at Wal-Mart.

I met my $17,000 spending requirement in less than a fortnight. Seems like a large amount, but it's easier than it sounds. All one needs are steady nerves and friendly cashiers. The former can readily be developed through training as with most other athletic faculties, while the latter isn't really up to chance. Cashiers are like mirrors; how they treat us is just a reflection of how we treat them, though you'd have to expect to come across a foggy or one-way mirror every now and then.

The next step was to liquidate the massive number of gift cards. For that, I needed make a pilgrimage to the Temple of Card Smithing, or, as it is more commonly known, the Money Center at Wal-Mart. Bill pay and money orders were my devotional rites of choice.

By the third trip to Wal-Mart, I had the procedure down pat. Walking to the high priestess, I mean CSR; I slipped over a credit card statement on which my name, phone number, payee zip code, and card number were circled helpfully in red ink. "I'd like to do a bill pay."

Carolyn was a cherubic woman with straight black hair tied back into a ponytail. In the early hours of morning the store was almost completely deserted, and she was the only person staffing the Money Center. I glanced at the back of the room and saw a king-sized mattress leaned up against the wall. "I didn't know you sell mattresses."

She punched a few keys on her side and then, holding the statement closer to her spectacles for cross-checking, continued data entry. "Not that brand," she said with a dismissive wave of the statement.

"Then why's it here?"

"Some guy tried to return it yesterday without receipts. A kind of shady guy."

"Shady?"

"Yeah, you know the ol' return without receipt scam."

"But you didn't fall for it, right?"

"Of course not, we don't even carry that brand." She looked up from typing. "Two thousand dollars even."

I invoked the secret incantation of the Mystery of Card Smiths. "Can you split that into four swipes, $500 each?"

The first two swipes went through without issue, the balance due amount sequentially dropped to $1,500 and $1,000. The payment terminal, however, took slightly longer than normal when processing the third swipe. In place of the usual congratulatory *Approved*, the screen now displayed *Not Authorized*, and the receipt printer spat out a cookie-fortune sized strip of paper: *Error 51*.

That glitch torpedoed the entire bill pay. Wal-Mart only allowed a maximum of four swipes per transaction, and having used three swipes I couldn't pay the remaining $1,000 with my $500 gift cards.

Giving Carolyn an apologetic smile, I ducked outside and called gift card customer service. As it turned out, the card was not properly activated, so like someone new on a job who didn't get the work memo, it didn't know that it was supposed to carry $500. To fix the problem, I needed to email in pictures of the receipt along with the card's front and back. Not a big problem. My brother had earlier solemnly told me of the first commandment of manufactured spending: Thou shall keep all active receipts—so every single receipt so far lay neatly coiled in a zip-lock bag at home.

Once home, I made my way to the bookkeeping binder. Picking one receipt at random, I glanced at the printed text and cross-examined it with the barcode number of the problem card.

Uh oh! There was no way to cross-reference them!

These gift cards came completely enclosed in a paper package. The receipts duly recorded the last four digits of the package's barcode, but that barcode had no relationship whatsoever with the numbers printed on the enclosed card. The packaging had long been thrown in the trash, and there I stood with a single problem card and 25 potential receipts.

I shook my head ruefully. If I had taken a few seconds to write the card's number on the receipt, this wouldn't have been a problem. Yet another rookie mistake!

The back of the card listed a website where the card balance could be examined and past transactions verified. I tried a Hail Mary pass and entered the problem child's numbers into the page. Nothing came back except for a few lines in bright red letters advising phone contact with customer service. Puzzled, I entered the number of a well-behaved card. It worked fine. The balance on the summary page displayed $0, while a table listed the card activation and Wal-Mart transaction in meticulous details.

I leaned back and signed.

Casting my eyes over the list of transaction once more, I had a eureka moment. Every single good card listed the activation time stamp on the webpage, as did the receipts. In principle, I could go through every single good card to collate its time stamps against the receipt. The one unmatched receipt at the end would belong to the problem child.

Half an hour of straightforward but tiresome toil later, I breathed easier. Good thing I only had to search through 25 receipts. If this had happened a month or two later, I would have had to search though hundreds. Believe you me, it got tedious fast.

Within two weeks of my initiation, the entire $17,000 was liquidated through Wal-Mart and Rite Aid. Seven thousand dollars went into bill pay, and the remaining $10,000 was converted to money orders, which then took up residence in my personal checking account, the same one that my father opened for me more than 10 years earlier as a high school graduation present.

Shortly thereafter, the phone rang while I was at work. Caller ID listed Unknown. I casually picked it up and put it to my ear.

"Hello, I'm calling from Bank of America fraud department," said a pleasant female voice.

The hair on my neck stood up while my heart sank. This wasn't going to be good. From that line alone I could tell why they were calling.

"There's $10,000 in suspicious deposits we'd like to talk to you about."

In the silence of the lunch-time office, I could hear a dull lub-dub sound growing louder. It was my own heartbeat!

"Uh, yes. I k-know about those . . . deposits," I stammered.

"Oh good, did you deposit them yourself?"

"Uh, yes?"

"May I know the reason for the deposits?"

"I'm, umm, starting a business with . . . my cousins." Goosebumps rose on my hands while I groped about making things up as I went along. "We're pooling f-funds together in my account for now."

"What line of business are you thinking of?"

"Um . . . entertainment?"

"Are your cousins the source of the deposit?"

"Yes. We need to make a large purchase of . . . instruments soon."

"Do you plan to make further money order deposits on your personal checking account, sir?"

"No ma'am!"

"Well, that's all I need. I recommend that you open a separate account for your business."

She cleared the fraud alert and hung up. I put the phone down. Tiny beads of sweat were glistening on the black glass screen, where it had come into contact with my face.

Yet another rookie mistake! Lucky for me, the CSR bought the story, even though it had more holes than a golf course. My brother's advice came floating back into my mind: "Don't eat where you crap." That was the first and the last time I used my personal checking account for card smithing. That role, as time went on, belonged to tempered throwaway checking accounts. As a well-respected card smith put it, "Who doesn't have five checking accounts?"

The biggest rookie mistake was yet to come. A few days later, judging that my credit scores were ripe for harvest, I sat down for my card hunt. Casually pulling up my credit profile, I gazed at the summary screen.

The score on the screen came out like a beanball and nearly knocked me out of my chair.

In place of a number in the mid 700s, the screen displayed 670, well below the minimum margin for lucrative bonuses. Somehow my Giving Tree had withered when I wasn't looking. I wondered if vandals had gotten to it, or if I had forgotten to prune and water.

Some frantic digging in the report revealed the cause of the precipitous nosedive. I had let the American AAdvantage card go to the end of the month with $7,000 outstanding balance on a $10,000 credit line, making for a utilization-to-credit ratio of 70 percent. Even though I was still in the 30-day grace period, the high utilization ratio flagged me as a borrowing risk. I couldn't blame the credit score models, though. My profile probably fit most warning signs of a risky borrower: quick jump in credit card balance, high usage ratio, and a flurry of recent card applications.

I leaned back and smiled at myself. What a mistake-riddled start! At least the problem was easily fixable. All I had to do was to pay off the balance and the score would correct itself.

When the next month rolled around, the miles were duly deposited into my frequent flyer accounts—100,000 for American, 15,000 for United, and 30,000 for US Airways— which we later put into good use for two round-trip tickets to Europe plus one domestic round-trip.

WORKFLOW IN PROGRESS

I SPENT THE NEXT FEW DAYS thinking very hard about how to take advantage of my newfound knowledge. From where I stood there were two roads: one towards the travel hacker hamlet and the other the cashback camp.

After some soul searching I decided against the former route. Our miles balance was more than enough to keep pace with our wanderlust (in economy class, at least). Going further into travel hacking meant more business and first-class redemptions, or carrying large savings in frequent flyer miles. My wife and I had no interest in the former, and the latter was like holding money in German banks after World War I.

I set about looking for cashback cards, and 5 percent cashback rose to the front as the target of choice. At the time, there were two cards of note. The first came from Wells Fargo, available nation-wide and promising 5 percent cashback on grocery, drugstores, and gas for six months after opening an account. TD Bank offered the other, giving 5 percent cashback for six months on dining, groceries, and gas, though it was only available to customers living on the east coast where TD Bank had operational footprints. Both cards were uncapped, so in theory the only limit on the cashback depended on how much I could spend within six months.

I still held out hope for an uncapped cashback card not subject to limited-time promotions. There were cards offering 6 percent cashback on groceries, but they capped the annual bonus-eligible spending at $6,000. That's not even enough for one afternoon's work. Other cards provided unlimited cashback for groceries, but the rate was fixed at only at 3 percent. After several days of trawling online forums and blogs, I slowly became convinced that an uncapped 5 percent cashback card was the philosopher's stone of this age—wildly lucrative and at the same time nonexistent.

One night, I sat up reading discussion threads in FlyerTalk's Manufactured Spending forum until deep into the night. Inside the room there was no sound save the clock's mechanical ticking, while outside the window the sound of crickets reverberated incessantly. Next to me Delilah lay sleeping, blissfully untroubled by the worries of the card-smithing world.

Diving deep into the archives, I came across a thread named Old Amex Blue. It lay innocently among neighboring threads with topics of consequences like CVS, Kroger, and Amex gift card. I glanced at the title briefly before continuing on to a thread on the latest rumor of CVS and their cash-only memo. Faint wispy recognition darted on the edge of memory, but I paid it no heed.

Half an hour later, the name Old Blue Cash blazed across my mind. I had seen it earlier! In another thread describing the cashback "Hall of Fame" cards, I saw that same name. Next to it was a terse description: "First $6,500 at 1 percent cashback, 5 percent unlimited cashback thereafter at grocery stores, gas stations, and drugstores. Discontinued."

Even as early as a month before, I would have dismissed the card as pedestrian, but after my forays to Wal-Mart I read the same description as: "Apply here for license to print money." How fortunate it is that the bonus categories—grocery stores and drugstores—are precisely the place to buy gift cards! If I'd had that card, I could have made $40 net profit for every $1,000 of gift card. Too bad it was discontinued. I remembered shaking my head as I read the hall-of-fame list, ruing how I always seemed to be one step behind the times.

I quickly backtracked to the Old Amex Blue thread. Not knowing what to expect, I clicked on the link. Perhaps it was a discussion thread on the glory of the old days, or maybe even a forum for grandfathered users. It wasn't unknown for threads to remain in limbo for years after the passing of the instrument of interest. The page loaded slowly. Its blue navigation bar and banner came on first while the rest of the page seemed to take its time.

Hallelujah!

Right in the center of the page was a backdoor link. Even though the card was officially discontinued, somehow someone had figured out that opening a certain link while setting the Internet browser to private mode will bring up an application for the card of legend, the great living fossil of a bygone age. And the same terms applied—unlimited 5 percent cashback at grocery stores, gas stations, and drugstores!

Wide-eyed, I looked up from the computer. The heyday of the cashback craze had long passed into memory, and yet this fabled card lurked here in the deep like a coelacanth. I really didn't understand Amex and their generosity, and I probably never would. The card was likely leaking money like a pin-holed water balloon, and yet they still allowed its continued existence. Some mysteries were just beyond mortal understanding, I guess. Hands slightly shaking, I shot off two card applications (both approved), and went to sleep dreaming of oceans and sky. Outside the cricket continued their songs of glorious spring.

The next morning, I went on recruitment. "How'd you like to come and work for me?" I asked Delilah.

She gamely went along with it. "Are you starting a business?"

"Yup. I'm going into gift cards."

Her eyes laughed. "You're making me a partner, right?"

"Nope, you have to start at the bottom and work your way up."

"I'll think about it. What are the duties?"

"You know, going to Ralphs, Vons, CVS, and Rite Aid. Wal-Mart too, of course."

"Hours?"

"Evenings and weekends. Pretty much on-call all the time."

"How about the pay?"

"Nothing."

"Medical and dental?"

"Nope and nope."

She leaned back and regarded me suspiciously. "You know, that is a horrible gig. Your company sounds more like a sweatshop."

"But it offers a very good retirement package."

"Can't be that good."

"Plus three weeks of vacation per year anywhere in the world."

"*Anywhere* anywhere?"

"Your choice of destination. Airfare, hotels, and all expenses paid by the company."

Her laughter lit up the room. "Where do I sign up?"

In the next few weeks, I devoted myself to building an infrastructure for moving funds through the Old Amex Blue. The three main avenues for liquidating gift cards were money orders, bill pay, and prepaid card loads. Of those three the first two were no longer viable options. Bill pay at Wal-Mart, for one, did not allow payment to American Express and my primary checking account remained off-limit to money orders. Thank goodness for the Serve Cards.

The Serve Card is a sibling of an American Express prepaid card called the Bluebird, whose popularity give rise to the phrase "feeding the birds," meaning to load gift cards at Wal-Mart. They are practically mini-checking accounts. Both cards allow the cardholder to make deposits at Wal-Mart's cash registers (called *loading* in smithing parlance) to the tune of $5,000 per month, payable in either cash or debit (code for gift cards). Once funds are loaded onto the Serve Card, they can be used to pay major credit card issuers (including American Express) electronically via the built-in bill pay feature. A long-time staple for the recreational manufactured spenders, the Serve Card offers the ease of loading at Wal-Mart, along with the expanded inventory of payable billers. Another benefit of the Serve Cards is that they are eligible for the occasional American Express Sync Offers, but that's a story for later.

I immediately opened two Serve accounts, one each for Delilah and myself. One week after receiving my two Serve Cards, I'd already maxed out the $10,000 total monthly load capacity and once more searched for means to enlarge my money pipeline. The Game had taken hold, and it was addictive! Ten thousand dollars per month was nowhere near enough to quell the card-inspired restlessness.

Delilah noticed my distraction. "What's on your mind?"

I explained how meager two Serve Cards were the rate-limiting factors in the inchoate gift card business. She furrowed her eyebrows and shook her head in amusement "How much did you do this month?"

"Only $10,000."

"Aren't you limited by the credit lines?"

"What do you mean?"

"You know . . . I thought you can't spend more than your maximum credit lines per month."

I chuckled and explained that a credit line simply is a limit on the maximum debt outstanding at any single time. That number is more like a moral suggestion than an unbreakable taboo. Any good credit smith can funnel payment back onto the card within a few days of purchase to free up the credit line again through a practice called *credit line cycling*. My credit line, for instance, was $7,000, which could easily be maxed out within a week. However, if I sent payment into the card as soon as the purchase charges come in then the credit limit would be renewed and available for abuse, I mean use, again.

She listened to the minutiae patiently if somewhat disinterestedly. "Still, isn't $10,000 enough for you?"

"Not even close."

My dour looks earned me a snicker from Delilah. She patted my hand, but she clearly understood *not* my restlessness. No one did.

An idea occurred to me. I had approached this all wrong. "I made $400 in profit last week," I added casually.

The twinkle in her eyes changed from amused to amazed. "Really?"

"Really."

"In that case, want to use my sister's name? How about my parents'?"

That was a great idea! We pooled our heads together and identified family members who were amenable to lending us their identity. After some horse-trading and arm-twisting, we opened four more cards. With the six Serve Cards under my control, I could load up to $30,000 per month at Wal-Mart.

Once I got a free lease on new identities, I opened four new Amazon Payment accounts. The service allowed sending $1,000 from credit cards per month per account. Initially, I used the Fidelity Amex card (2 percent cashback) as the funding source for an easy $120 profit per month. Eventually, I found an even better card—a Japanese card—that gave 3 percent cashback on everything. Being a foreign network card, it had about the same acceptance rate in America as a college application of a straight white male with a 3.5 GPA and no extracurricular activities. But all that mattered was that Amazon Payment accepted it. Six thousand dollars flowing in a circle worked out to be $180 profit. Soon channeling my payments in a circle became my favorite activities at the end of the month.

My phone chirped late one night. It was my brother and it was urgent. He had bought a $500 gift card a few hours earlier only to find that it was a ticking time bomb.

The card activation had gone properly, so the card had the full amount ready for use. However, the magnetic strip was tampered beyond repair. Someone had opened the gift card from its packaging while it was still in the store, recorded the card information (16-digit number, expiration date, and CVV value), disabled the magnetic strip, and resealed the card to its original packaging. They probably were checking the balance daily and were poised to drain it if they found anything.

Poor Harry was basically stuck in a jungle with the killer rabbit of Caerbannog downwind. He couldn't do bill pay or Serve load at Wal-Mart because of the tampered barcode, and he'd already used up his monthly Amazon Payment quota. In principle, he could have contacted the card issuer and complained, but that route meant paperwork and extra eyes.

"Calm down," I said. "Send me the card number and expiration date."

"You still haven't done your AP sending?"

"I do it at the end of the month."

"Why?"

"Because of things like this."

A few minutes later, the $500 evacuated from the tampered card into the refuge of my bank account. Glory be to Amazon Payment, beloved to all card smiths.

"You can wire me the money whenever convenient."

"I'm afraid I can't do that, Harry."

"What, why?"

"You're getting paid in gift card."

His approving laughter echoed from the phone. "You learned well, my padawan."

Of course I learned well. Though newly initiated, I had already mastered an aversion for cash (Second commandment of smithing: "Thou shall only pay cash as the last resort"). Cash payment doesn't qualify for cashback, and no card smith likes to leave money on the table. If our wives were kidnapped and held for ransom, we'd probably ask to pay the ransom in debit gift cards, and failing that, ask if the kidnappers would consider taking a money order.

The last buttress of my architecture came in the form of Serve credit card loads. An extra but very welcome bonus, the Serve Cards, like their predecessor the Bluebird cards, allowed funds to be loaded onto the account from a credit card. No fee necessary. Regular Serve Cards could load $1,000 per month, and those opened in conjunction with Softcard—a phone-based digital wallet service–had a higher monthly capacity of $1,500. It was basically a license to print money in its purest form. I could load $1,500 per month onto a Serve Card from a

2 percent credit card and earn $30. A few days later, I'd go back and do a bill pay from the Serve onto the original card.

In principle it was similar to Amazon Payment when it came to fee-free credit card spending. However, while Amazon Payment accepted new funding source with about the same standards as a community college admission department, Serve required an exact match of the account holder's name, SSN, and address. Authorized user cards were not allowed (trust me, I tried).

Not too long after this, Harry discovered a great workaround, which he implemented to great effect on his nine Serve Cards. Capital One was offering a certain business credit card with a flat 2 percent cashback. Through the online banking interface, the primary cardholder could order authorized employee cards that were uniquely associated with the employees' names, SSN, and work address along with a unique 16-digit card number. These employee cards passed the stringent Serve verification with no problem. Further, by linking all nine Serve Cards to the corresponding employee cards, he could manage the monthly loads and payment from a single credit card profile.

Two months into the manufactured spending game, my workflow was humming, churning through $35,000 per month despite still being incomplete. The Serve credit card loads and Amazon Payments were done from the comfort of home. Wal-Mart also went along swimmingly. Perhaps it was the early hours, but the employees that I encounter in my early morning stops tend to be cheery, mostly patient, and willing to go out of their way to be of help. One cashier even taught me the register keys for starting the money loading process (Press 70 then Action Code, swipe Serve Cards, enter number one for Load, then follow on-screen instructions), so that I could walk greenhorn cashiers through. A few cashiers started recognizing me as a regular and initiated the card loading process by the time it was my turn at the register. .

Towards the end of the second month, strange things started to happen at Wal-Mart. In the past, a gift card swipe immediately triggered a PIN screen. For some reason, the card readers started to deviate from that script. After a swipe, it dithered for about a second before flashing the signature panel, only to immediately kick back to the payment prompt screen. Repeated swipes were unsuccessful, as were attempts at a different Wal-Mart. Reports of the issue poured into the manufactured spending forum, where we pieced together the picture. It was happening nationwide, but fortunately it was limited to variable-load cards from CVS and Rite Aid. The erratic behavior was limited to transactions at the cashier registers; attempts at Wal-Mart's Money Center Kiosk (Kate) worked as they should.

The problem, it seemed, stemmed from a software update that classified these particular gift cards as credit cards. The Serve money loads were hard-coded to accept only cash or debit; hence, the quick display of the signature screen along with the cancellation of the swipe.

The FlyerTalk community had the best card-smithing minds working day and night on the problem, and soon a workaround emerged. The key, apparently, was to change the payment type to *Debit* in the brief window between the card swipe and the signature prompt. The ancient point-of-service (POS) systems (monochrome black on green screens), required customers to tap on the *Cancel* button in the lower right corner of the screen and then tap on the *Debit* button that next appeared. This brought back the PIN prompt, at which point the transaction was on familiar ground. On newer POS systems with color screens, one had to press the yellow *Change Payment* button that appeared in the bottom middle and then press *Debit* to summon the PIN screen. The cashiers would then punch the *Debit* key on their end to finish the transaction.

Armed with the knowledge, I went back to Wal-Mart. A patient cashier and a few false starts later, I managed to hit the *Change Payment* button before the system cancelled the swipe. It was pretty tricky. The *Cancel* or *Change Payment* button only flashed for a fraction of a second, not to mention that some of the touch screen panels had the responsiveness of a sleeping college kid after pulling an all-nighter. To further complicate the problem, sometimes the cashiers immediately pressed *Debit* on their end before I had a chance to switch the payment type. Every such swipe was a mini press-a-mole game. The frequent journeys to Wal-Mart grew much more interesting, but it was the kind of "interesting" that I wished would happen to someone else.

Shortly after this I encountered trouble when attempting a standard bill pay ($2,000 split into four swipes of $500 each). The cash register refused to deduct the proper amount on each swipe. Reports of the same problem came from all parts of the country, and once more the community had the best money-smithing minds working on the problem. We soon found that another software update have hit the POS system, this time affecting the split tender system in an obscure part that mostly affected manufactured spenders while leaving mainstream customers oblivious. Previously, splitting a transaction on the register side required punching the *Partial Payment* key on the cashier's side before entering in the desired amount. The customer would then swipe the card, and the funds would drain accordingly. After the software update, the gift card needed to be swiped first so that the system could recognize whether the payment card was credit or debit. After that the cashier could press *Partial Payment* and deduct the right amount.

Surprisingly, no Wal-Mart cashier knew about the new split payment system. I had to train cashiers in the new system as time went along.

One early morning, I walked up to the Money Center. The cashier on duty was Debra, a gentle taciturn lady with horn-rimmed glasses with whom I had loaded the Serve Card once or twice but never a bill pay. We carried on anyway, and by the time she announced, "Two thousand dollars even," I was ready with my spiel about the new split tender system.

Before the first syllable got out, Debra removed her glance from the card statement and met my eyes. "Go ahead and swipe the card first, hon."

I was caught off-guard. "I think t-there's a change in the split payment."

"Jessie told me about the update. Said one of her regulars taught her. You must be that guy."

"How'd you know it was me?"

"He said the guy does $2,000 per shot and it's split into four swipes. Not many people fit that profile, you know."

After the transaction finished, Debra handed back the card statement and the receipt. "Be careful with credit cards, hon," she said kindly.

That was the first time I heard of my reputation as "that guy." The card smith in me wanted to remain anonymous and to draw as little attention as possible, but deep down it was gratifying to be known as "that guy." Friendly cashiers later told me of my other reputations. In certain stores, I was known as "the gift card guy," in others, "the miles guy," and in some stores "the strange guy." My favorite, though, was at the Ralphs near work, where I was known simply as "the guy."

One morning I loaded my Serve Cards with a new cashier. She was young and pretty with long blonde hair. Curls streamed over her shoulders and partially covered her nametag.

My card finished, I handed over Delilah's. "Can I load this for my wife too?"

She complied and pretty soon $1,000 left the confines of their plastic prison. "What's your name?" I asked.

"It's Mandi." She gazed down and then brushed the curls away. "These always get in the way."

I made a note to remember the name and waved goodbye. Another cashier walked by. Her name was Angela. "Loading money for your wife again?" she asked.

I grinned broadly, "You remember me."

"Of course, you're the guy who always loads money for his wife."

"Yes ma'am."

"You were here last week. Your wife must spend a lot."

"Yes ma'am."

Mandi and Angela exchanged a knowing look. I didn't know what they communicated, but I knew they were on the same page. As I neared the door I caught a snippet of their conversation: "I wish my man did that for me."

A few weeks after the software updates, my brother called me at night. "Gift cards no longer work at Wal-Mart," he said, his tone dead serious.

Shocked, I immediately rushed online where reports from like-minded brethren were surging in from all corners of the country. The situation was indeed serious, though not quite as dire as I thought. Variable-load gift cards from CVS and Rite Aid, the same ones that had been behaving erratically after the software update, no longer worked at Wal-Mart. (Technically, only the debit feature stopped working, but that's the only worthwhile feature). Gift cards from other grocery stores, being issued by different banks, continued to work without incident.

We card smiths sure live in interesting times.

I rushed to the computer and pulled up my spreadsheet to assess my exposure. There were only six cards in stock for a total of $3,000. I breathed easier. It could have been worse.

"How much exposure you got?" I asked.

Harry responded with a text containing a picture of a stack of gift cards, still in their packaging, neatly piled into a stack three inches high and banded widthwise with a rubber band. "Still 14k left," the text read.

Fortunately, other avenues remained opened. Over the next month, I liquidated my remaining stock through a combination of Amazon Payment, utilities payment through EvolveMoney, and buying money orders at Rite Aid. Online, there was panic galore for people who exclusively relied on that card issuer. Old timers living in rural areas with only access to CVS and Rite Aid fretted about the loss of income. Newbies fearfully posted questions on alternative routes for cash-out as the card closing date loomed.

Recriminations broke out between fractions of the community; the heavy hitter blamed the airline bloggers for publishing the secrets of the game; the recreational manufactured spenders blamed the heavy-hitters for excessive antics bringing undue attention from gift card companies. A few posters vainly appealed for unity and calm, while fewer still observed sagely that change was inherent in the nature of the Game. Bend with the flow, they suggested.

In between the din, my brother and I busied ourselves diverting gift card purchases to Ralphs, Vons, and Albertsons while around the country our comrades rerouted purchases to their local grocery stores. It was a sea change in the landscape, but we adapted accordingly. Although the river of manufactured spending had encountered a boulder, it simply flowed around the obstacle and streamed on, recrimination and grumbles notwithstanding. As water always seeks low ground, the heart of a card smith always strives for profits.

Two months into this upheaval, my brother sent another image over the phone, this time of 28 gift cards strewn haphazardly on a desk. "All drained," the text read, followed by a smiley face.

By the time the dust settled, my workflow stood whole and complete. Every month $50,000 in gift cards flowed through the Old Blue Cash (4 percent net cashback). Another $7,000 moved through the Serve credit card loads (2 percent net) while $6,000 went through Amazon Payment (3 percent net). Total monthly profit was $2,300.

This smithing life ain't bad.

ERRORS AND HICCUPS

IT WAS LUNCH TIME. I SAT in my office scheduling online credit card load for the Serve.

Delilah rang. I glanced at the phone wondering if she had finished loading her Serve Card. Across the street from her workplace was a Wal-Mart, and that morning I packed her $2,000, along with her lunch.

"I'm at Wal-Mart and there's a problem."

I sat straight up in my seat. Harrowing scenarios loomed darkly. "What problem?"

"The register didn't take my card swipe."

"It couldn't read your card?"

"No, not that. When I asked to load $500, the cashier pressed some button, and then a receipt printed."

"That's it?"

"Yeah."

"What does the receipt say?"

"It said $500 was loaded, but I didn't swipe any gift card."

Phew . . . this wasn't too bad. At least it was an error in our favor. I had an inkling of what went wrong. "Did the cash register pop open?"

"Umm . . . I think it did."

"Then I know what happened. Your cashier pressed the *Cash* button instead of *Debit*."

"Er ... in English please?"

"Just that Wal-Mart thought you paid in cash instead of card."

"So what do I do now?"

"Depends. What's the cashier doing?"

"There's a manager trying to undo the load. But he'd been at it for ten minutes."

"Is there an ATM nearby?"

The phone went silent except for a faint echo of Delilah conversing with the cashier. She soon came back. "Yes there is."

"Withdraw $500 from your checking card and give it to the cashier. That should balance the register."

"Are you *sure?*"

"Yup, it's the right thing to do."

That night, she came home with two big bags. "Well?" I asked.

"That worked out. I gave them the cash, and the cashier was happy as a clam." She raised her hands. "Guess what I got?"

The blue Wal-Mart name and the yellow starburst logo adorned the bags. Through the mostly transparent plastic I saw what looked like clothes. "Hmmm . . . you went shopping?"

"Bingo!"

I chuckled. "That's not how it works. It's like taking one step forward and two steps backward."

"But you said we made $80!"

"True."

"Live a little, you know."

She disappeared into the bedroom to try the clothes. I saw a white triangular piece of paper peeking out between the folded creases like a little cat's ear. It was the receipt. I reached out for it . . . but changed my mind halfway. Smiling ruefully I filed away the drained cards. Oh well, I'd just make an extra trip to the grocery store.

"Ta-dah!"

I looked up to see Delilah reappear in a pretty blue dress. I nodded appreciatively. "It's lovely."

She twirled. "You got any more cards? I can go load tomorrow."

"Er . . . I'm okay. I can go load myself."

"You sure?"

"Yeah, I don't want you to . . . er . . . waste your precious lunch hours."

<hr>

The path of money smithing is long and never smooth. If complications, whether arising from vagaries of the card gods or self-inflicted, were hurricanes, then card smithing would be the Caribbean in September. As far as hiccups go, what Delilah encountered was a mere baby twister, more amusing than dangerous. Rarely a month goes by without newbies on FlyerTalk posting questions on how to retrieve funds locked away from situations gone awry. It could get quite serious, like the time one poster threw away six drained gift cards, only to have $3,000 in payment reversed (to those same cards) after his credit card got cancelled. Another fellow I know once had $4,000 in Wal-Mart bill pay reversed when his credit card issuer shut him down. The funds returned to Wal-Mart, but he had already thrown away the bill pay receipts and had no way to prove he was the rightful owner. Yet another fellow I know once bought several thousands in gift cards in the days after the great Wal-Mart Card Purge. Having failed to keep up with the news, he stocked up on the wrong gift card brand and had to spend the next several months spending them down through every day expenses. Most of the time, however, complications arose from purchases not activating properly or cards being compromised, and woe be unto those who failed to keep the proper receipts, for their lot are the rending of garments and the gnashing of teeth.

One of my closest calls came at Ralphs. Vacation was looming, and I hurried about in the morning buying as much as I could. So much money, so little time.

June helped me with the purchase. "Haven't seen you for weeks," I commented.

"I've been on vacation."

"Oh, where?"

"Florida and a cruise to the Caribbean. Lovely weather right now."

"Which port did you go to?"

"Went to Belize and Cozumel." She added nostalgically as her hands flew over the keyboard: "We're been looking over the vacation photos every day."

"And wondering where the time went, right?"

"Yeah."

June and I shared a smile. I knew trip nostalgia only too well. The signature screen came on, and I signed it while still engrossed in conversation. One great thing about card smiths is that we don't have a vacation wish list; we have a vacation backlog. The Caribbean was on my list right behind Europe and Hawaii; I'd been eyeing Belize in particular because I heard they had some of the best snorkeling in the world.

The receipt took a bit longer than usual to print, and when it finished out came two items, the receipt and an activation slip. June glanced at the activation slip and raised her brow. "That's weird," she said, sliding it over. "Not activated," went the bad tidings.

I took out my other Old Blue Cash card. "Let's try that again."

Same error this time. June handed me another faulty activation slip. Both transaction receipts she cached below the screen next to the keyboard.

I apologized to June and walked back to the car feeling puzzled.

Briefly I considered driving to work, but a subdued prickling uncertainty hung in the air like the sword of Damocles. Something was off, though I couldn't quite put a finger on it.

Turning off the engine, I called American Express customer service.

A pleasant voice came on. "How may I help you?"

"I just had a purchase declined, and I want to clear the fraud alert."

The customer service rep went silent for a few seconds. "How long ago was the purchase, sir?"

"No more than ten minutes ago."

"There's no declined transaction, sir."

"That can't be, I was there!"

"My records show a $1,011.90 charge a few minutes ago at a Ralphs. No declines."

In the frigid morning, I could feel goose bumps rising on my neck and arms. My cards had been charged!

Images of the signature screens came back like a freight train. My mouth felt agape in horror. Both transactions already went past the signature screen, and so as far as Amex was concerned I owed them $2,000. The air was stifling as I sat pondering the situation. Most likely something had gone wrong on the gift card activation network. The gift card company now owed me $2,000, but I didn't have a single shred of paper to prove it.

I hightailed it back into the store faster than an Apple fan on iPhone release day. Bearing onto June's register like a madman, I wheezed, "Did you . . . huff . . . keep the receipts . . . huff . . . from those transactions?"

She stared at me with eyes widened.

"Y-yes," she finally spoke. She pulled the receipts from beneath the register. "Been thinking of throwing it away just now."

I seized the receipts. Each listed a balance of $1,011.90, and the bottom half showed the details of the payment card—card issuer network, card number with the first 12 digits replaced with asterisks, and most reassuringly, a line at the bottom listing a reference number for the transaction.

I clutched the receipts as relief came flooding. Without them I was like a spelunker trapped in a cavernous hole, a $2,000 hole, with no rope or any foothold along the sheer vertical slope and with the dark closing in. With the lifeline in hand the climb outwards was uneventful, though by no means uncomplicated.

Charles the manager was initially unhelpful, but a quick three-way conversation with American Express customer service convinced him that my cards were indeed charged and that the funds had gone astray en route to the gift cards. He processed two refunds, and 10 minutes later handed over two updated receipts showing that the funds had been found and repatriated. "Give it two or three business days for the pending charges to reverse," he said.

I mumbled my gratitude and Charles waved it off pleasantly. "We could redo the card purchase if you want," he offered.

I politely declined.

Hiccups at the cash registers are by and far pretty seldom. More frequently complications—judging by my own experience and the numerous SOS posts online—involved activation issues and unauthorized gift card charges. There were two ways to deal with the latter concerns. The dumb way was to work through the card issuer complaint channels. The smarter way was to complain to someone else—the government, preferably.

Not too long after I started, three gift cards refused to work at Wal-Mart. Swiping them at the POS terminal resulted in the infamous *Error 51* declines. Customer service told me that they were not properly activated because someone had tried to access funds on the cards six months prior when the cards were yet to be purchased. He asked me to fax over a letter with a cover sheet describing the problem, along with images of the cards' fronts and backs, and pictures of the receipts. They'd get back to me within ten business days, he concluded.

There was nothing but the sound of crickets over the next ten days. I called back on the eleventh. The representative was sympathetic, apologetic even, but unhelpful. "I see no notes on your account. Give it a few more days," he said.

I inquired if there was any record of my fax, but he had no way to check that information.

"Can I talk to the Loss and Prevention department?" I asked. No can do. I requested a manager, who was similarly apologetic and helped me file an escalation request.

"Someone will call you back within 48 hours," he promised.

That assurance was about as good as Third Reich's promise not to invade Poland. On the third day, I called back only to be met with another information impasse. They did help file an escalation request on the previous escalation request though. I didn't hold my breath waiting for a phone call, and it was a good thing that I didn't.

I faxed over a scathing letter threatening to sue in small claims court if no action was taken within the next five business days. That too seemed to have disappeared into the ether. Nearly a month after discovery, my three gift cards were still useless empty husks despite the two faxes, two escalation requests, over ten phone calls to customer service center. I was no closer to my $1,500 than when I discovered the card compromises. It was aggravating.

When the deadline for my small-claims threat passed, I was fuming harder than the Titanic's smokestack. I spent several evenings researching agent of service and litigation procedure, and soon I had a small-claims form filled out and ready for dispatch.

Delilah noticed the seething irritation. "Anything wrong, hon?"

I gave her a quick briefing. She tilted her head to one side. "Isn't there a better way than suing?"

"I tried everything."

"Did you try being nice?"

"Nice, reasonable, angry, pleading . . . tried them all."

"Escalating to managers?"

"Too many times to count."

"So why can't you get the phone reps to fix it?"

"They're slippery like eels."

She pursed her lips and looked skywards. "I have an idea. Doesn't hurt to try."

I called and immediately escalated to a supervisor. Laurie listened politely to the situation and reiterated the familiar refrain: "I see notes that they're working on it, Mr. Doughsmith."

"Can you just transfer me to Loss and Prevention?"

"Sorry sir, I have to go through the proper channels."

"But it'd been a month already."

"I'm sorry, sir."

"I heard that plenty of times already."

"I could file an escalation request."

"Come on, I already tried two escalations."

"I understand, sir. I could expedite the escalation request, if you'd like."

Time to try my wife's little trick. "Can I get a record of this conversation, Laurie? Like an ID number."

A slight pause. "I don't have a conversation ID number, sir."

"Maybe like a customer service ID number?"

She read off her customer service ID number. Her voice was stony.

"Thanks Laurie. Can you help me put a note on this account?"

"Yes, I can do that."

"Can you write down that I talked to you today?"

"Sure."

"And that I will now sue in small claims court?"

"You know, I may be able to get you Loss and Prevention."

"Oh?"

"It's unorthodox, but I can use the company private message system. Someone will call you back soon."

Two days later, a young woman from the Loss Department called back. She asked for the store addresses, time of purchase, and the reference number, all of which I passed over the phone. No silly faxing required. "The cards are cancelled and new cards will be FedExed to you within two days," she said matter-of-factly. A whole month of angst and ire, and yet all it took was ten minutes over the phone with the right person to fix it.

Three new gift cards arrived in the mail in due course. I keep their now empty shells separately from other drained gift cards as mementos of those angst-filled days.

The next time that I encountered compromised gift cards was immediately after my second trip to Europe, though the trouble began before our departure. The three-week trip mandated a break from gift cards, but I was dead set on maintaining my monthly $50,000 quota. Vacation was no excuse to leave money on the table, though it's not an easy thing to do when one only has nine days. Every single day was spent at either a Wal-Mart or a Ralphs, and by the time the airline 24-hour check-in email arrived, I had only managed to funnel $35,000 through Wal-Mart.

I did reach my $50,000 purchase quota—that was the easy part—but I still had $15,000 in gift cards outstanding. Taking the gift cards to Europe was out of the question, and yet leaving them in our unoccupied home seemed to be a precarious proposition. It was too late to open a bank safety deposit account, and my family probably would flip if I went to them with $15,000 for safekeeping. A nerve-wracking if somewhat rare dilemma, it was.

In the end, I decided to chance it and hid the $15,000—peeled and arranged into a playing card-sized deck about 1.5 inches high—on the inside of an air-vent slot near the basement with a liberal application of scotch tape. I didn't tell Delilah about it, though. Before we left the house, she took a tour checking to make sure that all locks were securely latched. She even rattled the door knobs and the window latches for good measure. "I still don't feel safe with the TV and computers inside," she confided as we carried our luggage outside.

I tried to keep an even expression. "It'll be fine. We've got neighbors watching the house." I thought it best not to tell her that if thieves were to break in and steal everything else (TV, sofas, computers, refrigerators, etc.), their combined values still would have been less than that one little card deck hidden inside the air vent.

When I opened the door to the house three weeks later, I made a beeline for the air-vent slot. There, much to my relief, the cards lay physically undisturbed.

I fired up my computer and checked the card balance one by one. Three cards had been compromised while I was traipsing around the Old Continent. One had already been completely drained of its contents in two charges: one exploratory charge of 99 cents, and another cleanup charge of $499. The other two cards were in various stages of electronic thievery. One silver lining was that all charges were made at online purveyors. Those counted as credit transactions and were much easier to reverse than debit card-present transactions (don't ask me how I know).

This time around, however, I was more than prepared. The dreadful experience from the last whirl on this merry-go-round had motivated me to do extensive research, from which I learned that it was more expedient to make a nuisance of oneself outside the company's usual complaint channels.

I filed card replacement requests and waited ten business days. No response, though I wasn't really expecting any. Once that passed, I fired off a complaint to the Better Business Bureau (BBB) and for good measure threw in a Consumer Financial Protection Bureau (CFPB) complaint. Within a week I received a solicitous call from some woman in the Prepaid Department. She expedited the replacement process over the call and even offered to overnight new cards to my address. The bank responded in writing to the BBB complaint with an apology—a 180-degree switch from indifference to deferential. It went to show that in this line of work, a well-placed complaint is a problem almost solved.

Several more bouts with compromised cards convinced me that that BBB and CFPB complaints (and FDIC when it came to checking accounts) are the Holy Hand Grenades of Antioch for manufactured spenders. Simply pull the pin and count to ten days—no more, no less—and then lob it towards the bank in dispute. I have to admit that I do get a bit gleeful whenever filing one of these regulatory complaints. I get a mental image of the prepaid dispute center employees diving into the trenches for cover whenever one of these Holy Grenades come flying in. An explosion (accompanied with a hallelujah) rattles the ground and rubbles fly indiscriminately. Dirt-splattered employees poke their heads out cautiously and then dash about to rectify the situation before another Holy Grenade comes soaring. While this picture is probably only partly true, I do get much satisfaction, perhaps a bit too much, at lobbing these regulatory explosives. The angst and ire from the early days probably ran deeper than I thought.

That brings me to one of the strange side effects of the gift card business—the tiny uncertainty that lies in the space between the swiping of a card and the *Approved* message. Unless a card has been brought or verified within hours, there is always the possibility that someone had already compromised and drained the card, leading to a card denial at the cash register—an embarrassing event, I assure you. The chance is fairly remote (and dependent on the card issuer and denomination), but the law of large numbers has a way of catching up when one goes through more cards per month than a professional poker player.

But to be honest, I do cherish the moment of thimble-sized anxiety as I swipe a card at the cash register. It makes me feel alive. On the rare occasion that a card is rejected, my heart sinks, and I dart out of the store to verify the remaining balance. But most of the time the swipe goes smoothly, the moment being a little bit sweeter because I had pulled the slot lever and won.

In truth this Game is like a *Bizarro World* version of the Las Vegas slot machine, except that here the odds are stacked against the house. Most pulls result in tiny $5 to $20 payout, and the whole goal is to avoid hitting the *Error 51* jackpots.

TRAVEL HACKER SWISS KNIFE

WITH THE WORKFLOW FULLY CONSTRUCTED, I started paring away the superfluous routines, streamlining my way towards moving $50,000 per month in as few hours as possible. My childhood fascination with completing a video-game racing course as fast as possible manifested itself in numerous hours optimizing with my gift card routes and Wal-Mart runs. There was always some area that needed to be refined, whether it was dovetailing my visit with a favorite cashier's schedule, or timing a bill pay to free up the spending limit before the next grocery store run. Eventually, I managed to bring the total hours to about 40 hours per month, mostly early mornings and weekends. Sounds like a lot, but when you're having fun that time just flies by like a shadow of a falling leaf on the windowsill.

Everything seemed to be going my way. Delilah enthusiastically came onboard after sitting down with me once or twice as I redeemed the end-of-month cashback. Her initial skepticism was no match for the persuasive powers of seeing $2,000 extra income showing up in our checking accounts per month. She now even suggested making a detour to pick up gift cards whenever we go out (happily accepted) or to load the Serve by herself at Wal-Mart (tentatively accepted). Out of the blue, American Express also sent me an email raising my Old Blue Cash credit limit. "To recognize your excellent history as an American Express credit member," it read, "the credit limit of this account has been increased to $16,000." To cap it all off, I had just set a new personal record.

Feeling boastful, I rang up my brother. "I just hit my best month ever. Guess how much."

"Sixty-five k?"

"Not even close."

"Eighty k?"

"Yup, eighty-one k. Been working especially hard this month."

"Eighty-one k is your best month ever? For me it's just April."

No rain was going to stop my parade. "This manufactured spending hobby sure is addictive."

His voice bubbled with merriment. "So you feel the card itch too."

"I wish I had known about this years ago."

"Enjoy the Old Blue Cash while you can. It won't last."

"Why?"

"I've been in this game a long time," he said ruefully. "Deals always come and go."

"Seems pretty stable last few months or so."

"Did you forget about the Great Card Purge of Wal-Mart?"

"Okay, except that one."

"And EvolveMoney going with the four cards per month limit?"

"Okay, except that one too."

"You should have seen the old days. Some credit cards used to give 10 percent cashback. And I used to get 15 percent off on gift cards from Staples. Just before you started, I was buying Vanilla Reloads at CVS on credit, and in those days you could load the Serve at CVS *with credit cards.*" His voice waxed nostalgic. "Those were the days."

"You mean Old Blue Cash won't become Old Faithful?"

"Ha, you wish."

I shook my head. "Nothing can replace the Old Blue Cash, though."

"You just need to diversify. Manufacture spend a mile wide and an inch deep, you know."

I hung up convinced of the need to diversify. Apparently, money cycling routes are like Floridian sinkholes: they open and close all the time, often without warnings. My current workflow was a mile deep but an inch wide. If the Old Blue Cash were to die tomorrow, I'd be going cold turkey! Scary thought.

***

After surveying the credit card landscape, I settled on the Chase Ink Bold as a complementary card to the Old Blue Cash. The card offered 5 percent back in Chase Ultimate Rewards points for purchases at office supplies stores, up to $50,000 per year. Moreover, at the time it was possible to sign the card up for the Visa SavingsEdge program, which gave an additional 1 percent cashback for purchases over $200 at Staples.

Technically, Chase Ultimate Rewards points could be redeemed for statement credit at one cent per point, but savvy travel hackers redeem the points through Chase's online hotel, flight, and car rental booking service for a higher rate of 1.25 cent per point. Most importantly, however, Chase had partnerships with multiple airlines and hotel, allowing Ultimate Rewards points to be transferred to a host of frequently flyer programs like United, British Airways, and Southwest airlines (all my favorites), in addition to a host of hotel programs (not so favored). To top off the sundae, the Chase Ink had a promotional bonus of 50,000 points for spending $5,000 within three month.

Within two weeks three Chase Ink Bold cards came in the mail, two for me, including an authorized user card in my name, and one for Delilah. The cards were deep blue with the word *Ink* etched across the front in flowing calligraphy, and staring at it I could feel that we were going to be best friends. Unlike dating, with credit cards one could always tell at first glance whether the relationship would work. However, just like dating the cards are liable to change midway into a relationship and become unrecognizable from the happier days.

After online activation, I took it to the nearest Staples to scope out the landscape. Entering the store for the first time, I took stock of the layout and, guided by the invisible attractive force emanating from gift cards, gravitated towards the prepaid racks. Contrary to the vertical set-up in grocery stores, these cards lay on slots on horizontal cascading shelves. No variable-load card was in sight. The maximum denomination was $200.

I stood at the gift card rack and mentally cranked the numbers. The gift card fee was $6.95 per card, so $1,000 in gift cards cost $35 in fees. This amount was bit steep, but being able to transfer to United, British Airways, and Southwest more than justified the cost. At a semi-conservative estimate of 1.5 cents each, that worked out to be an effective 5 percent net cashback, yielding a profit of $400 for $8,000 spending per month. I could live with that.

"Find everything okay?"

I glanced up to see a kind smiling face, one stripped of the inexperience of youth yet not yet burdened with the wrinkles of age. The top of his nametag read Chris, and the bottom displayed Store Manager. His beaming smile struck me. It was the kind that one has when happy, not the kind to convince someone else of happiness. I grabbed 10 gift cards and waved them. "Sure did."

The sole cashier on duty was occupied so Chris waved me to an empty register. "Buying them for your business?"

"No, I buy those to get miles on the credit card."

"That's a good idea!" He ran his finger along the ridges of the cards, his lips moving wordlessly as he counted. "Register has hard-coded limit of $2,000 per transaction. I'll have to split these into two purchases."

"Sure"

"I'll need your ID, of course."

"No problem. Are these cards popular?"

"Not so much. There's a lady who buys 10 per month for her business, though."

I tried to suppress a smirk. Twenty bucks said that her business was in travel hacking.

Next time I came I bought my wife along, and we each grabbed $2,000. Between the two of us we cleaned out the fixed-denomination $200 cards from the shelves. When Sarah the cashier saw the heap of 20 cards in our hands, she leaned into the intercom. "Need help opening up a register."

She was a tall, slender, girl with raven-black hair. Reaching for a card, she flipped it over and started pulling off the perforated tab from the long end. The paper tab was finicky. Most of the time it tore off in the middle, and she had to pick at the ripped edges to resume removal.

I reached for one. "There's a better way to do it."

Flipping the card so that the tab faced upwards, I put my thumbs about two inches on either side of the tab and then with my index and middle finger applied pressure from below. The tab snapped upwards, revealing the barcode below.

Sarah raised her eyebrows. "That's a nifty trick."

"I've worked with a few gift cards."

After all cards were scanned, she leaned into the PA. "Manager to the front register, please." Meeting our eyes, she waved at the register. "I need the manager key for anything over $400."

Chris swung by, "Did you guys just clean out all my gift cards?"

"Guilty as charged. Sorry."

He inputted his supervisor code and turned to Delilah. "Hello there. You must be the lady he's taking all over the world."

"If I'm not, he's in big trouble." She shook his hands and they got along famously.

Sarah finished scanning in the second batch of cards, and Chris typed in his code once more. Shaking my hand before leaving, he nodded in Delilah's direction. "Bring her along next time." He winked. "She's a lot more fun to talk to."

Remembering something, he turned to Sarah. "There's a memo about a band of women going around with stolen credit cards. Call for me if anyone tries to buy gift cards, regardless of amount." He waved a finger in my direction. "Don't worry about this guy though. He's okay."

Within a few weeks we got up and running, diverting about $8,000 per month from the Amex Old Blue Cash onto the Chase Ink Bolds. Liquidating the forty $200 cards per month was much more troublesome as it called for many more swipes at the register. Fortunately, the tender splitting process at Wal-Mart worked wonders. Most cashiers got a hang of it quickly, and together we choreographed a new variant of the manufactured spending waltz. I'd ask for $600 to be loaded.

The cashier would enter $200 and press *Partial Payment*. I'd swipe. Cashier would enter $200 again, and once more around we would go, twirling gently in lockstep. A few Wal-Mart cashiers worked out my loading patterns, so that no prompting was necessary. If the load amount was $500 or $1,000, then they would split the payments into multiples of $500; if $400, $600, or if it was $800, it would be split into multiples of $200.

My mileage game went up several levels with the addition of the Chase UR points. The improved liquidity bypassed several of the more annoying limitations of frequent flyer accounts. For instance, I could reset the expiration clock for United MileagePlus indefinitely by transferring in nominal amount of Chase UR points. The best thing was that with the reliable harvestable UR points from Staples, I was no longer dependent on airline-specific card bonuses to accrue miles.

When one of my best friends, Shawn, got married, I offered my expertise in airline miles for honeymoon planning. If he applied for two credit cards, one each for him and his wife-to-be, then I would guarantee him two round-trip tickets to either Hawaii or Europe, making up for the shortage of miles from my own pool if necessary. They chose to go to neither, but eventually settled on Japan and Thailand for the honeymoon.

"I'm short 10,000 United miles," he called one day. "Got any way to fill the gap?"

"How urgent do you need it?"

"Within a month or two."

I shook my head, "Too late for card applications then."

"Yup."

"You should've talked to me earlier, man."

"I've been using the United MileagePlus card for everyday purchases. Thought I could make it but guess not."

"You planned to do $10,000 in spending to earn 10,000 miles?"

"Well, yeah."

I nearly rolled on the floor laughing. Eventually I managed to stop, "What's your MileagePlus account number?"

Pulling up a browser and logging into the Chase UR portal, I transferred 10,000 miles to his account. "Done. Enjoy the miles."

"That's it?"

"Yup, don't forget to book a stopover for an additional free flight."

I caught myself as I was about to hang up. "Almost forgot something. Chase technically only allows transfer to my own airline account or my spouse's."

"What does that mean?"

"It means if anyone from Chase asks, you should say you're my domestic partner."

"Done."

I recouped the 10,000 points on the next visit to Staples, where Delilah and I once again cleaned out Chris's stock of $200 gift cards. Shawn eventually booked round-trip award tickets to Japan and Thailand, stopping in Japan just in time to see the fleeting cherry blossom season. The Thailand-Japan leg was free (a huge additional saving) because he utilized the free stopover feature of United's awards program.

On occasions when car rentals are necessary, Chase UR points are my go-to choice for booking because the discounts can go as high as 50 percent off. When I was planning for Hawaii, I looked for car rentals everywhere but couldn't find rates below $70 per day. Even AAA membership didn't have much traction. Imagine my surprise when I logged into Chase and was able to find the same car rentals at $45 per day from their specialized travel booking service. I'd long known that big companies like Chase had more leverage and more influence on price than small-fry like me, but the generosity of the savings it was willing to pass on floored me. Even better, Chase UR points could be redeemed at a rate of 1.25 cents per point, bringing my effective rental cost down to about $36 per day. Like many travel hackers before me, I quickly came to regard the Chase Ink card to be one of the most treasured and the Chase UR program to be indispensable. If travel hacking were survival camping, then the Chase UR program would be a Swiss knife. If travel hacking were the French military force, the Chase UR program would be the white flag.

Not long ago, I dropped by the airport to pick up my sister Fiona. She too had wanderlust, but unlike mine hers wasn't suppressed under stinginess. Like the rest of the Doughsmith family, she knew the price of everything, but unlike her brothers she also knew the value of travelling. On this particular trip she and her friend Jen were returning from an East coast trip.

"How was the trip?"

"Great. The flight back, though, not so much."

"How so?"

"We're in the last boarding group and, surprise, there's no overhead bin left."

"You should have applied for an airline card. They give you 'boarding group two.' Right after elites, woman with children, and military members."

Fiona turned to Jen and whispered, "He's a credit card geek."

"Oh my gosh," Jen said, "My brother is just like that. He has like ten credit cards."

"Really?"

"And he's always going on and on about miles and such."

My ears perked up. "Miles, you say?"

"Yeah, one time my whole family went to London. He insisted on paying the check-out bill with his credit card and had us pay him back in cash."

I placed myself in this brother's shoe and mentally ran through the list of major travel-hacking cards. Maximize hotel category bonus and avoid foreign transaction fee. "Was it a blue card with the word *Ink* on it?" I asked.

"Oh my gosh! How did you know?"

"I recognize a lion by his footprints."

ONE CARD TO RULE THEM ALL

LIFE WAS GOOD. EVERY MONTH $50,000 flowed through Wal-Mart while another $10,000 or so flowed through online credit card loads. For everyday spending I had a wallet brimming with category-specific cards. The Old Blue Cash gave 5 percent cashback only on groceries, drugstores, and gas, but I had the best available cards for the remaining popular categories: 5 percent on books, 4.2 percent on airlines, 3 percent for restaurants, 5 percent for office supplies, 3 percent for Amazon, and a 2 percent general-purpose card for the miscellaneous if frequent remainders. Rounding out the wallet was a Chase Freedom card that gave 5 percent cashback on three categories of Chase's choosing that rotated every three months.

Something was missing. The whole operation was still incomplete, still imperfect, though I couldn't quite put my finger on the cause.

One night I went out for Chinese with my four best friends and Scot (he is listed separately because he only counts spouses as best friends). We had a tradition called "annual trip," a yearly guys-only vacation that so far had taken us to New York, Chicago, Sequoia National Park, Boston, and Washington DC. Spouses or significant others were not allowed, and, after a disastrous experience, neither were casual friends who wanted to tag along for sightseeing. Our destination and schedule for the next trip were topics dominating conversation as of late.

"I got good news," I announced.

"Do tell."

"The whole country is our oyster now. I can guarantee tickets for anywhere within continental US for $250 per person."

"What's the catch?"

"There's no catch."

"We know you. There's always a catch."

"Okay, maybe except for an occasional red-eye flight, sitting in cattle class, or going through an ungodly number of connecting flights."

"This is your mileage thing, isn't it?"

I grinned broadly. "Yup."

"Spill the beans. Why so generous?"

"Let's say that I've found a new mileage supply. I'm no longer dependent on card applications for miles."

They looked among one another and nodded. It was the kind of nod you do when you're too polite to shake your head.

"I'm telling you guys, you should get into this game. Banks are handing out free money everywhere."

"It's not free money, Jaime."

"Yeah, there's no such thing as a free lunch," Dustin added.

"Remember Amazon Payment I told you about? You could set up accounts among yourselves and send money in a circle. With a 3 percent card you could get $30 per month."

"Sounds like too much work," Logan observed.

"It only takes 10 minutes per month, man."

"Nah."

I slightly shook my head. If there was another way for the average Joe to earn money that easily without coming out a lesser person, then no one ever told me. Still, I wasn't their keeper.

Dustin picked up a piece of dumpling. "Well, since we're on miles, I'm thinking of going to Europe."

"When?"

"About two months from now. Can I buy miles from you?"

We fired up our cell phones and searched airline prices. Round-trip tickets were going at $1,800. With so little advance notice I could book the same flights for 90,000 miles plus $150 in taxes and fees.

"I'll give you my miles for 1.25 cents each. Let's just round your whole cost down to $1,250. If anyone else wants to buy miles, I'll also give you 1.25 cents each."

Peter put up a protesting hand. "Whoa, how come you're charging a premium on those miles?"

"I'm not charging a premium."

"You just charged one cent per mile for the annual trip."

"True, but I'm operating at a loss in both cases. Miles don't grow on a tree, you know."

"But I know it cost you way less to get the miles."

I breathed a sigh of exasperation. "You know, if you strongly object to it then you're welcome to buy miles from airlines instead. They're happy to sell you miles for three cents per mile."

Dustin raised his hands conciliatorily. "Hey guys, I'm okay with saving $600."

We shook hands on it.

Shawn turned in my direction. "By the way, Beatrice and I are planning a trip soon."

"You want to buy miles too?"

"No, we need to borrow camera equipment." He rolled his eyes diagonally upwards, "What's that thing you use to take pictures remotely?"

"Tripods?"

"Bystanders?"

"Selfie sticks?"

"That's the one. Selfie sticks."

I waved my chopsticks dismissively. "No self-respecting photography enthusiast would ever use a selfie stick."

"Get with the times, dude."

"Yeah, selfie sticks are all the rage these days," Dustin added as he picked up another piece of dumpling. "It's considered *de rigueur*."

"You say 'de rigueur.' I say 'amateur.' Potato, potahto."

Shawn shrugged. "Anyways, can I borrow your stick, Jaime?"

"You can borrow my tripod. Delilah's got my stick."

"I thought she only got your balls."

We burst into raucous laughter that brought alarm and raised eyebrows to neighboring tables. I grinned broadly while shaking my head. It was the kind of shake you do when approving nods aren't enough. "Touché, buddy. Touché."

I reached for my wallet when the server came by with the check. Restaurants . . . that fell under the Chase Freedom rotating categories for the quarter. Rifling through the various special category cards, I eventually found it and plopped it on the table.

I looked around and saw that three people on the table had also taken out their cards. All were Chase Freedoms. I bobbed my head in approval. "You guys know the special category for this quarter."

"Of course, 5 percent cashback for restaurant, department stores, and Starbucks. Who doesn't know that?"

I pulled the card back and let the guys jostle to be the one paying. Shawn ended up with the bill, which he paid with his Freedom, and we reimbursed him in cash.

We continued the conversation at a dessert place famous for their smoothies. It was a small mom-and-pop place: the kind where you order at the register, and then they call your name when the order's ready. When it came time to order, I stepped up to the counter and glanced around the shop. A few tables for waiting patrons filled the layout of the shop and in one corner board games lay available for all to borrow.

No server and no sit-down menu were anywhere in sight, so the store probably was classified as Confectionary or Misc. Food. That meant I'd have to use my 2 percent general purpose catch-all card. I flipped open my wallet butterfly style and rifled through the list. Everyday spending cards occupy the entire left hand side. Holding each card in turn, I ticked off the categories: grocery, gas, office supplies, Amazon, etc.

Hmmm. this was weird. My general-purpose card wasn't in the stack. I searched through the list again. Found it this time. The sneaky little fella was hiding behind the Sallie Mae card.

Ah ha!

This was the reason for my discontent. No wonder my workflow always seemed incomplete. I'd been walking around with the financial equivalent of a 40-part screwdriver kit, switching out the head bit every single card transaction. It didn't really sound like a lot, but the weight of the entire toolkit could really be a drag. Life was too short to be fiddling around guesstimating each store's merchant code and rooting through the wallet for the right card. There's got to be a smarter way of doing this.

Smiling, I handed the 2 percent cashback card over for payment. My friends, I noted, paid their post-prandial treats with the Chase Freedom, which only received 1 percent cashback at the store.

That night, as I shelled gift cards in preparation for Wal-Mart, the answer came to me. It was right in front of me all along. I'd been playing with the answer every single day and, in fact, I had a plastic tub in the garage full of them. Gift cards! I already got them at 5 percent off thanks to the Old Blue Cash, so if I used them for everyday purchases I could essentially transfer the Old Blue Cash's grocery stores' bonus to everything else. My hands were too short to give myself a pat on the back, so I folded them and bobbed my head in self-appreciation instead. It was so simple it was strange no one else had thought of it. Or perhaps I had mastered money cycling faster than I thought.

I dialed my brother to flaunt my ingenuity. "I've thought of a way to get 5 percent cashback everywhere."

"Okay, try me."

I laid it out.

"That's a stupid idea," he said flatly.

"What . . . why?"

"Because you're just trading one set of inconveniences for another."

"No I'm not."

"Look, you have to pay inside whenever pumping gas."

"Fine, except that one."

"And you'll have to carry multiple gift cards and track their balances."

"True."

"Not to mention cashiers and servers. They're pretty suspicious of gift cards."

"Well . . ."

"Listen to me. I've worked a lot with gift cards. I trust them about as far as I can throw them."

"But you throw like a girl."

"Exactly!"

I breathed a sigh of disappointment as my ego deflated. "Oh well, back to the drawing board."

"No need. You've come to the right place."

"You mean you know a card with high percentage everywhere?"

"Yeah, 5 percent cashback everywhere."

I was wounded. "You had the Holy Grail, and you never told your own little brother?"

"You never asked."

He outlined the general principle. These cards were prepaid debit cards similar to the Serve Cards. Unlike the Serve, however, these cards could be used for PIN-based purchases—such as buying money orders at the Post Office—because they were on Visa and MasterCard networks. They could not be reloaded at Wal-Mart like the Serve; instead, funds could be deposited into the prepaid balance via reload packs that were purchasable at grocery and drugs stores (cue the entrance of the glorious Old Blue Cash). PayPal cards could be reloaded with PayPal My Cash (purchasable at Rite Aid and CVS), while T-Mobile cards could be reloaded with Reloadit Packs (purchasable at Vons and Albertsons). Both reload packs have a fee of $3.95 per $500 card, but that fee is refunded through either additional cashback or fee reimbursement, giving them both 5 percent cashback everywhere Visa and MasterCard are accepted! In principle, Harry's technique also worked by transferring the Old Blue Cash's 5 percent rate at grocery stores and drugstores to everywhere else. Unlike my scheme, however, his wasn't limited by the disadvantages of actually using gift cards.

As I typically do with new financial instruments, I sallied forth to find reliable sources for PayPal My Cash and ReloadIt cards. The former were easy; CSV and Rite Aid were happy to take credit cards for thousands of dollars without even blinking an eye. ReloadIts were much harder. I hunted high and low within a 10-mile radius of my home, and found only one grocery store that wasn't insistent on a cash-only policy. It was a Vons that by some quirk of fate also happened to be the same store where I bought my first gift card ever, the first step in a thousand-mile journey through financial wild, wild west.

Since the first foray at Vons, my workflow had taken me to easier stores elsewhere and I hadn't been back for some time. The store remained the same as I remembered it. The reloadable section lay immediately to the left of the prepaid gift cards, where I could see the Happy Graduation gift cards that once made me sweat bullets at the register. Next to it were the Happy Birthday gift cards, and in the top row rested the generic non-occasion cards that I now favored. I smiled at the thought of a younger me perspiring under the (imaginary) scrutiny. There are some *fell things* to be afraid of in this line of work; cashiers are the least of them.

I plucked one ReloadIt card and took it to the cashier lane where Dawn, a woman with pretty curly hair cascading past her shoulders, obligingly initiated the fund-transfer ritual. She paused for a moment after keying in the amount ($495) and looked up. "Did you receive a threatening phone call?"

"Umm . . . no." I looked around. "Should I have?"

She held up the reloadable card. "There are a lot of scams with this card."

"Really?"

"One time I had an elderly lady come in to buy three of these. Someone called her about a bench warrant and that she needed to pay or be arrested. She was supposed to buy these and read the card numbers over the phone."

"That's criminal! Did you stop her?"

"It took some convincing but I did," she said proudly. "Told her to call the police station and confirm first."

I thanked her for her vigilance and continued on my way. It wasn't the first time I crossed the tracks of unsavory illegal schemes. Unfortunately, the same gift cards and reload cards we credit card smiths so prize are prime targets for those who sell their conscience piecemeal for a profit. For better or worse, scammers and manufactured spenders tread the same tracks. Both groups preys on their marks in secretive schemes for a quick profit, but the marks for the former are everyday Joes and grandmas, while for the latter the marks are the towering financial institutions. Scammers sell peace of mind and risk of jail for money; we exchange our financial literacy for profit. It all comes down to what happens at the end of the day. I don't know how scammers manage to sleep at night, but I, as a card smith, slumber soundly in the sleep of the just.

―――――――――――――――

With a steady supply of PayPal My Cash and ReloadIt cards, the dream of the one card to rule them all became reality, much to the relief of my wife who no longer needed to put up with lectures about using the right card for the right purchase. My wallet became much lighter as all special-purpose cards were relegated to the sock-drawer, where they shared a cozy space with the numerous airline cards. This one card was the capstone of my workflow. With it in place, I was finally a full-fledged and card-carrying manufactured spender with all the rewards, privileges, and hiccups appertaining thereto.

Words of my new prize scattered through my acquaintance circle like a ripple in a lake. A few weeks later, my college buddy, Jerry, called. "I need to purchase a business-class ticket to Edinburgh," he said. "Ticket price is reimbursed by the company. Help a brother out?"

We trawled the Internet looking for the most convenient direct flight between Los Angeles and Edinburgh. I knew Jerry.

If he were buying a ticket on his own dime, he'd be flying in "cattle class" at the most ungodly hours and going through more legs than a lost poodle in an aerobics class just to scrimp a few dollars. When the company was paying, however, money was no object. We constructed an itinerary with every ounce of convenience and comfort money could buy. The final price tag for the business-class ticket came out to be $3,500.

"I can get 5 percent off plus about 8,000 miles. You take 3 percent and I take the miles plus the 2 percent. How's that?"

"That's a bit steep for your fees, isn't it?"

I explained to Jerry that the 5 percent off doesn't magically gather in the ether like guardian angels and wait for a card swipe before taking wing. I'd need to devote about an hour to gather the necessary reloadable cards and several days to fatten my prepaid cards with the necessary funds. A 50–50 split was considered a loss, as I could easily keep 100 percent to myself after doing the same amount of work.

"Fine, but still . . ."

"If you want, we can flip it. I take the 3 percent and you take the miles plus 2 percent."

"No need. I'll take my $105 and call it a day." He hesitated a bit. "This is all legal, correct?"

"Absolutely. As far as your company is concerned, you produce a receipt and they process the reimbursement, right?"

"Yeah . . ."

"And if you never came to me, you'd probably book the same $3,500 flight, right?"

"Yeah."

"And they'd pay you back $3,500 anyway, right?"

"Yes."

"Open and shut case to me."

"Fine, book it and I'll write you a check," he confirmed before hanging up to tell his wife the good news.

Half an hour later, Jerry called back. "Does your cashback card work on mortgage payments?"

"Jerry, this card is the Leonardo da Vinci of payment cards."

"Er . . . why?"

"Because it works on everything."

He grew thoughtful. "I have a proposition for you," he said slowly. "How about you pay my mortgage every month and I'll reimburse you? Same deal, 3 percent for me and 2 percent for you."

My father once told me the second best way to lose a friend is to do business together. The airfare purchase was a one-off affair, but a recurring mortgage deal required responsibilities and liabilities that I wasn't sure I wanted impinging onto this friendship. "I'll make you a much better offer. I'll teach you to obtain the card yourself."

"Sold! You got yourself a deal."

I rattled off the main points for assembling the one true card. Apply for the Amex Old Blue Cash. Apply for a prepaid debit card. Buy reloadable packs at drug stores. Load funds onto the prepaid card. Wallow in cashback. Jerry took meticulous notes.

We dropped out of contact after that. A few months later, I happened to come across Jerry. "How did it go?" I asked.

He shook his heads, "Never got around to it."

"Really? . . . Why?"

"Too complicated."

I never inquired further, though I didn't really understand his financial inertia. I am not his keeper, and it wasn't my business to badger him into earning a hundred quick bucks. But still! I practically made sure that he received the call of Easy Money, and yet he picked up the phone and said "wrong number." At the very minimum, he could have used the card to pay his monthly mortgage for a quick $125 profit. It would have taken an hour per month max. At his hourly pay rate, he'd have to work about four hours (six if you consider after-tax income) to make the same amount he could gain within an hour from the comfort of his own home. Why would he eschew the fast $125 per hour gig and yet, if summoned for overtime, happily toil away at a much-reduced hourly rate?

I wondered what was stopping him. Did he not see the Giving Tree for fear of the forest? Perhaps it was a discomfort with the unknown, or a sense of unease about walking too close to the dark, wandering in places where one is not meant to step. We all erect barriers in our minds in those regions where fear and discomfort tread. I have mine and apparently that was his.

TWO WEEKS IN THE LIFE

I OPENED THE MAILBOX AND OUT slid a haphazard pile of letters, bills, flyers, and unsolicited advertisements. Flipping through them perfunctorily, my fingers ran across two that I immediately recognized as credit card offers.

I casually fished them from the rest of the mail. Offers I received in the past included a card with 1.5 percent cashback, a card with 30,000 United miles introductory bonus, a card with 15 months no APR on balance transfers (but with a hefty balance transfer fee, ha), and a card with an introductory bonus of $100. Junk, all of it. My personal rule is never to apply for a card with less than $350 rewards, and few cards are honest enough to offer that.

Today's offers were different though. The ocean blue font on the front seized my attention immediately. American Express is the most generous and smithing friendly company on this side of creation. If I pick any random veteran card smith on the street and look through his wallet, then I am guaranteed to find at least one Amex cards. And if there's none then the unlucky fellow probably got mugged earlier. I tore through the envelopes and found two offers for an American Express Open Business credit card, one each for my wife and me. Each promised 75,000 Membership Rewards points for spending $5,000 within three months of the card opening.

I did a quick mental calculation. The Membership Rewards points could be redeemed through gift cards or statement credit for about one cent per point. Those two credit card applications would net me $1,500 if I wanted cash. These offers certainly passed my $350 minimum rewards rule with flying colors.

I furrowed my eyebrows and cupped my chin in my hand. It would be hard to convince Delilah to apply for these cards. My long-suffering wife had long ago resigned herself to having many credit cards in her name because the ample vacation itineraries didn't just pay for themselves. However, she did put a limit of one card in her name per quarter. That's a measly four cards per year!

I had already used up her card quota that quarter. This was going to be tough.

I turned the problem around for view at another angle. The Membership Rewards could be converted to $1,500 in cash, but they could also be transferred to a number of airline frequent flyer programs. From that list, the most important was the British Airlines Avios program, which had the best redemption rates for flights to Hawaii. Round-trip tickets from my hometown of Los Angeles to Hawaii cost a mere 25,000 Avios points per person, so the two applications translate to six round-trip tickets to Hawaii.

Bingo!

That night during dinner, I casually slipped them, *Inception*-style, into the stream of conversation: "By the way, honey, two credit card offers arrived in the mail today." I nonchalantly continued digging into my plate.

Delilah waited a few seconds and, seeing no detail was forthcoming, prompted, "So, what was the offer?"

"Better than average." I studiously poked at a piece of broccoli.

"Go on."

"It's a $750 per card offer. One for you and one for me."

"Is that good?"

I could barely keep my straight face. "Better than average."

"Okay then."

She returned to her plate. A few tense seconds passed by. I kicked it up a notch, "I'm planning to apply for one under my name."

"Sure." She tilted her head slightly and looked diagonally upwards. "Didn't you just apply for a card in my name last month?"

"Yes, I did."

"Okay then." She dug into her plate once more. The next few second strained by under the heavy weight of finality. "I read that it's possible to redeem the points for Hawaii flights," I ventured desperately.

Delilah pursed her lips and it was obvious I wasn't winning this engagement. I thought I could see a small twinkle in her eyes. Damn it, she was probably enjoying it.

I sighed. Time to fold. "Can I apply in your name?"

"How many round-trips to Hawaii?"

"Six. If we plan our dates carefully."

Her eyes really twinkled this time. "Fine, you can apply in my name."

Later, I sat down to prepare for the card applications. Like a hunter laying out tools before a safari jaunt, I methodically prepared an area at the worktable. The offers lay to the left of the laptop; on the right hand side, my black book of applications was opened to the last recorded entry. A pencil rested idly on the edge of the black book.

First, a quick check of our credit scores on a credit reporting website indicated that our scores were healthy and ripe for harvesting. Hers was a healthy 765 while mine was a slightly anemic 730. They probably would drop four to six points each after application, but would recover and be ripe for harvest again in a few months.

I opened my web browser and entered the credit card promotion code. The offers were for a business credit card, but I'd been through that rodeo many times before. My side business was smithing money from credit cards, so I figured that I could be considered a sole proprietor. The trick was to fill out the application as honestly as possible and hope that it would be approved. If this were a personal credit card, I'd have had no problem getting an approval with my income and credit score. The business card application, however, was a whole different animal and subject to different scrutiny.

Business Address and *Legal Business Name* were easy. I just used my full name and home address. *Industry Type?* That was harder. Agriculture, nope; Construction, nope; Retail Trade, close but not quite. *Finance/Real Estate*: this description was probably as close as I can come to money smithing. *Years in Business?* Let's see, roughly about a year. *Number of Employees?* Delilah was my sole employee, so that would be *Between 0 and 5*. *Annual Business Income?* About $20,000 per year, give or take. On the top left corner was a banner prominently displaying something about the interest rate, but I paid it no heed. I never do. No self-respecting card smith would ever carry a balance, and so we never worry about the interest rate anymore than Peter Pan has to worry about retirement contributions.

I filled out the appropriate fields, crossed my fingers, and clicked on the *Submit* button.

Score! Instant approval.

The corners of my mouth turned up with the smugness of a hunter right after bagging a buffalo on the Serengeti. Time to move on to the next prey.

I started a new application for my wife, who did not need to be present at the scene. I already had all her information memorized. (Heck, they'd probably take away my credit smith

ID card if I couldn't remember my wife's social security number). Success! Instant approval for her as well.

The hardest part of this game was over. On paper I still needed to spend $10,000 within the next three months to earn the bonus, but the delay between this point and the bonus was a mere formality.

About a week later, I opened the mailbox and found two nondescript white envelopes among the run-of-the-mill mail. My smithing Geiger counter started pinging, and I just knew that these were the awaited Business Gold cards. I flipped the envelopes in my hand, feeling the heft and tracing the contours of the margin for that familiar feel of plastic. The pliant resilience of a card-shaped region in each envelope confirmed their presence.

I tore the edge of the envelopes widthwise and tilted the openings downward. A few quick taps on the opposite end and out slid the cards wrapped in several printed pages, including introductory material, terms and conditions, and an advertisement for yet another American Express credit card, which I saw at a glance was only standard fare.

I activated the cards online and created an account name and password, which I recorded in the black book. If this were any other bank, I would have called customer service to place a large purchase alert. I often take this step because most banks' fraud-detection algorithms have the sensitivity of a Venus flytrap. On several occasions, my purchase of gift cards totaling $1,000 was denied at the cash register because the new credit card deemed the transaction to be a potential fraud. It used to be a hassle to call in to remove the block, but I eventually wised up and placed a large-purchase alert on new cards to give the fraud-detect code time to learn my spending patterns. Fortunately, no such preemptive measure was necessary here. American Express has the most smithing-friendly fraud detection algorithm there is, probably because Amex is geared towards affluent cardholders. In fact, I have seen people run more than their declared annual income through an Amex card per month with nary a fraud alert. I've also activated and immediately purchased thousands of dollars on a new Amex card without any hassle. I really don't get why they are so friendly, though I have a sneaking suspicion one or possibly more manufactured spending secret agents managed to infiltrate, *Manchurian Candidate*-style, the upper echelons of the American Express executive board, from which privileged position they were pulling puppets and setting into motion events for the betterment of card smiths everywhere.

When I took Delilah to the local grocery store a few days later, I made a beeline for the gift card rack. I reached up to the top of the rack where the variable-load gift cards hung from a metal hook. The standard fixed-denomination cards varied between $25 and $200, but they all carried roughly the same fee per card as a variable-load that can carry up to $500, which explained why the latter type is overwhelmingly preferred in manufactured spending. Taking care to keep the cards in the same order, I removed the first few gift cards in the front. From the gift cards now exposed, I ran my finger through each and located the cards with the latest expiration date. The newer the cards, the less chance for a security breach.

I did a few more checks to minimize my chance of buying lemons. A popular gift card fraud relied on compromising the barcode in the back of the card. When a card is checked out at the register, the cashier has to turn the packaging over and pull off a one-half by three-inch perforated tab, exposing a barcode printed on the back of the actual gift card. (The 16-digit gift card number and expiration date were printed on the front of the gift card, which faced forwards and therefore remained hidden). The cashier would then scan the barcode, thereby activating the gift card with the appropriate funds. I'd heard reports of criminals who would take two gift cards off the rack and somehow remove the cards through small precisely inserted slits on the side of the paper packaging. They would keep one of the gift cards in their possession and duplicate its barcode onto a sticker, which would be pasted onto the other gift card. The tampered card would then be replaced in the packaging, resealed, and returned to the rack. When an unsuspecting customer bought the tampered gift card, the barcode on the sticker would be scanned, which would then activate and fund the card in the fraudster's possession. The unlucky buyer would then have a non-activated card in hand and a steep climb up the complaints process to be made whole again.

Fortunately, it is easy to distinguish the texture and appearance of the authentic barcode from its ersatz counterpart. They have slightly different reflectivity and texture. Tilting each card at an angle, I squint at the slot to verify that the barcode was indeed printed in glossy ink over the PVC plastic (the authentic ink has small scintillating spots that shift in response to changes in angle of view), and then run my index finger over the slots to feel for the uneven texture of the barcode as it varies between the alternating black-and-white vertical stripes.

Satisfied with their condition, I handed four of them to Delilah, who stood staring bemusedly. "Two different transactions, one thousand on each."

"Sure thing. Which lane?"

I scanned the checkout lane and found a familiar face on lane five. "Let's have Kristin check us out."

One of my regular cashiers was Kristin, a happy-go-lucky woman in her middle age, who always greeted her regulars like long-lost friends. Her name tag indicated that she had been with Ralphs for over twenty years, and given her natural aptitude for customer service, I thought it a crime that she wasn't occupying a higher position in the service chain. Once after I'd accumulated about $20,000 in purchases at her register, she looked at me and smiled.

"Why do you keep coming back for these cards? Are they for your business?"

"No," I said, "I buy them for myself."

When she gave me a funny look, I thought it best to explain before she summoned the cops. "I buy them for the airline miles," I said. Ever since then, the entire store knew me as "the miles guy." On a few occasions I have walked up to an unfamiliar cashier at this same store who, noticing I had three or four gift cards in hand, would say, "Oh, you're that miles guy." It's nice to be notorious.

My wife came up to Kristin and flashed a big smile. "Can we get these four cards in two transactions of five hundred dollars on each?"

There was a strange look in Kristin's eye. It reminded me of the look of someone about to deliver bad news to a friend. Before she was able to say anything, the cashier from the next lane over pivoted and ominously crossed the few steps to join our lanes. Her name tag identified her as Shift Supervisor.

"I'm sorry, ma'am. You can only buy these variable-load gift cards with cash."

I shot a glance at Kristin, who returned a sympathetic look, the kind that said she was sorry and liked to help, but the situation was out of her hands. I tried a Hail Mary pass: "But I was just here last week and I was able to buy with a credit card."

"It's a new memo from corporate headquarters. You can still buy them if you have cash or debit."

I ruefully slid the Business Gold back into the wallet. "Never mind then."

"My hands are tied," she said apologetically. "One lady wanted to buy $4,000 for a school last week, but we couldn't sell to her either."

"Wait, did you say some lady tried to buy $4,000 in gift cards for a school?"

Her face was serious. "Yes, sir."

Though despondent, I tried my hardest to repress a smirk. The odds of that lady buying gift cards for a school were about the same as the Jacksonville Jaguars winning the Super Bowl. I'd bet good money that she was in the same business as me, though she certainly won in the creativity department. I tapped on Delilah's hand and gestured back towards the gift rack. There we put the cards back, and upon passing Kristin on the way out of the store, I managed a wan smile.

The "cash only" update was earth-shattering news—about a solid eight on the Richter scale. The very life forces that sustain the manufactured spending ecosystem are card perks and incentives, and for that I need to be able to buy gift cards with credit cards. Lost in reverie, I plodded back to the car. Ralphs was my main source for gift cards at the moment. The four Ralphs around my home and the one near work supplied me with $40,000 in gift cards per month, and it would be incredibly difficult to shift that amount of spending to other grocery stores like Albertsons or Vons. I had established long working relationships with many cashiers at Ralphs, most of whom I saw more often than I see my best friends. Furthermore, Ralphs was the chain with the most liberal gift card policy. It was easy to buy $2,000 worth in two transactions, whereas other chains I was familiar with required managerial override for any purchase over $500. Now that Ralphs was no longer accepting credit cards for gift cards, my current profit would be taking a huge hit. And then there was the issue of establishing new relationships with cashiers at new stores. I could, however, funnel some of the purchases into Target stores to reduce the need for gift cards. . . .

Squeeze.

Awakening from my reverie, I saw that Delilah had taken advantage of a nearby curb to lean up and wrap her hands around me in a bracing hug. "Let's grab a pizza from Tomato Joe's over there," she whispered. I nodded distractedly, my mind still preoccupied with reconfiguring my workflow to direct $40,000 in purchases through alternative channels.

We placed an order for pizza and sat on the patio outside watching people walk by. I sat pensively contemplating the end of an era. Delilah was also silent. While she did not fully understand the implications of this tectonic shift, she was cognizant of its impact on me.

I wrote a quick text to my brother: "Went to my favorite Ralphs today. Cash only. Manager said it was due to a new corporate memo."

Hell, this was a bad day; I needed something indulgent. I walked alone to Ralphs and bought my favorite treat—cookie crunch gelato. Normally I avoided sweets, but heartbreaks merited an exception. I rejoined my wife at Tomato Joe's, and we shared the pizza and gelato together in silence.

"So, remember that time in Venice where we sat on Saint Mark's Square at night watching the orchestras?" she asked thoughtfully while nibbling on a spoonful of gelato.

"Umm, yes."

"And we saw a couple who sat down on the outdoor café and asked to look at the menu?"

Memories of the scene came back and the gloomy atmosphere lit up with a ray of *schadenfraude*. "Yea, when they saw the prices they stood up as if their seats were on fire."

She nodded. "Can't blame them though. If I saw sixteen euros for a cup of cappuccino, I'd be out the door too."

"Yup, the Venetians sure know how to jack up their prices."

Memories of the carefree days abroad started to dispel the heavy mood, and I could feel a nascent smile swelling. I should count my blessings. The Game had been good to us both. For a long while I had been making more than the annual federal poverty line for a family of two while working about 40 hours a month outside my normal eight-to-five. Not only that but we got to see most of Europe at an age where we actually had the energy to experience the hell out of it. If the Game were to end tomorrow, I'd still be way ahead. But the Game will survive. We card smiths are an inventive, cunning and hardy lot, and in the end we will abide. I grinned and said, "Regardless, I love Venice. Such a beautiful city."

"Sure is," she nodded wistfully.

"Remember that time we ordered a thirty-two-ounce beefsteak to share in Florence?"

"That *bistecca fiorentina* was worth every penny. I still can't believe that we drank a whole liter of wine along with it, though."

"You know, when we walked outside after that meal I wasn't sure I could find the way back to the hotel."

We guffawed at the crazier memories. At this point, my cell phone chirped. I glanced at the screen and found a message from my brother: "They misunderstood the memo. Ralphs' memo said that only purchases above 2k require cash only."

The clouds lifted. The glorious status quo still reigned! My Ralphs workflow was still safe, at least for a bit longer.

Delilah and I dug into the remainder of the gelato, which had become a celebratory treat. The half-drafted contingency plan moved from the *Emergency* folder to a dusty cabinet in the back office of my mind.

I later researched Ralphs' memo in a Kroger-specific thread online at FlyerTalk—my go-to destination for all things credit-card or frequent-flyer related. The relevant text of the memo read: "All purchases of open loop cards (Visa, Mastercard, Amex) are restricted to a maximum of $2,000 (including fees) in a single transaction and in a single day only. Single transactions over 2,000 (including fees) must be completed at the customer service desk. All transactions over $2,000 must be paid for using cash only." The consensus among card smiths was that transactions under $2,000 could be done at the check-out lanes and that credit card would be accepted.

Armed with this information, I sallied forth with Delilah a few days later to a different Ralphs. We again selected four gift cards each (after due-diligence security measures, of course), and joined Matt's check-out lane. Yet another one of my favorite cashiers, Matt was a stout, good-humored man who, in physical dimensions and personality, was a dead favorite at any Santa Claus pageant. I always went his way whenever he was staffing a lane. When we first met, however, he refused to sell me gift cards because my driver's license had an out-of-area address. Matt deemed the combination of a large purchase and out-of-area driver's license to be unusually suspicious, and I had to return a few days later with my work badge and a water bill that listed my name and local address. Matt burst out laughing when I showed up at his lane with my credit card, driver's license, work badge, and utility bill in one hand, and four gift cards in the other. Those documentations earned me the right to buy gift cards and Matt's lasting friendship.

He reached for the card packages. "Back again so soon? Do you ever buy anything except gift cards?"

"Of course we're back. How else are we supposed to account for half your store's gross revenue?"

Matt guffawed and with no prompting ran the eight cards in four transactions of $1,000 each. He knew the procedure well. There was no mention of any policy change or memo.

"So, where're you planning to go next?" he asked.

"We're planning a trip to Europe again. Three weeks this time." I swiped my American Express Gold Card. Seeing the question in his eyes, I added, "We're thinking of Berlin, Paris, Madrid, and Lisbon."

He glanced upwards as if he were mentally registering those cities on a map. "Oh, you gotta drop by Amsterdam. Be sure to visit their 'coffee shops'."

"What's so special about Amsterdam's coffee?"

"Beats me. Never tried their coffee."

"I thought you just said 'coffee shops'."

"In Amsterdam coffee is sold in cafés. Coffee shops are where they sell their famous . . . um . . . herbal products."

I made a mental note to add Amsterdam to the evolving itinerary. In the end, Matt handed us a plastic bag with eight gift cards totaling $4,000 and a tangle of receipts, coupons, and activation slips. We each had bought $2,023.80 on the Gold card (the gift cards had $5.95 activation fee per card), so we were two-fifths done with the spending requirement.

We bid Matt farewell and drove to another Ralphs, where we grabbed another eight gift cards and lined up at a checkout lane staffed by a cashier I had only seen once or twice. She probably was new. Delilah placed the four gift cards in two separate piles on the conveyor belt, separated from one another by the lane divider. The divider coincidentally had the words *American Express* in white text against a blue background.

I glanced at the cashier's nametag. "Hi Sheryl, can we get these cards on two different receipts?"

She hesitated. The poor woman probably didn't know whether we were a money-laundering Bonnie and Clyde duo, or an extremely rich if deceptively under-dressed couple. She shot a glance towards the next register for guidance, whereupon Adam emerged and joined our checkout lane. Toweringly tall with gentle bearing, he was a shift supervisor but his boyish face belied the managerial authority. He immediately recognized us and flashed a greeting grin. "Go ahead and sell to them, Sheryl. He's here all the time."

Sheryl picked up the card and started tearing off the perforated tabs on the back. Again, no mention of the policy change or corporate memo, so it looked like management of this Ralphs also passed high-school reading comprehension. She scanned the barcode and looked up. "How much on the gift cards?"

"Five hundred dollars on each, please."

Sheryl complied and we quickly added $2,000 to Ralph's daily gross sales. My wife came next. She gave the gift cards to Sheryl, flashed her winning smile, and said: "I love your hair, Sheryl. I wish I had curly hair like yours."

Sheryl beamed and it was obvious that Delilah just made her day. While Sheryl scanned the last batch of cards, Delilah picked one of the donate-one-dollar-for-charity barcodes next to the register and slipped it over. "Could you add this to the transaction too?"

I chuckled to myself. That's Delilah for you: one part Dale Carnegie, one part Mother Teresa.

We called it a day and drove home with a grocery bag containing $8,000, buried in a thick stack of paper packaging and paper receipts. A few days later, I finished off the remaining minimum required spending before going to work.

Ten thousand dollars in spending accomplished in 10 days. I was really off my game.

Fast forward a few days, I sat in my smithing office, more colloquially known as the corner of my bed. I needed to prepare the $10,000 in gift cards for a trip to Wal-Mart so that the funds could leave their plastic dungeons and make their ways through various means towards the credit cards from which they originated. If the gift cards were migrating salmon Wal-Mart would be their home river.

The gift cards in their packaging lay on the bed next to my bookkeeping binder. The laptop lay in the center, its browser opened to a spreadsheet where I keep track of the minutiae of *fund flow:* how much was spent on each of my ten credit cards (now twelve with the inclusion of the Business Golds), how much were already deposited into my numerous reloadable prepaid cards (think of these of mini-checking accounts), and how much was still floating in the form of gift cards waiting to make the loop. A trash bin had been placed within convenient tossing distance. Next to the binder were a pencil and a zip-lock bag full of rubber bands.

With an economy of motion that came from long practice, I liberated the cards from their packaging. You may laugh, but one needs to be efficient when one has 100 cards per month to process. The procedure was simple. Flip the package upside down so that the barcode faces upwards. Press the right thumb squarely on the back of the card while the left thumb secured the bottom edge of the package. The index and middle fingers of the right hand would then apply pressure upwards from the package's underside, snapping the package in half along the upper edge of the perforated slot. Fish the card from its paper enclosure and peel away the pieces of adhesive gel binding it to the packaging. Flip the inside flap of the package to reveal a four-digit personal identification number (PIN), and write the number on the card itself. The adhesive gels would be pasted onto the discarded packaging, and the entire thing would be tossed into the nearby bin.

I opened the bookkeeping folder to the plastic pocket divider labeled *Receipts*. The receipts, rubber-banded into a coil with the purchase dates written prominently on the outside, went into the divider, where they would stay until the next month when the gift cards were long spent. The first commandment of manufactured spending was "Thou shall not throw away active receipts." No adherent of the craft would dare violate this command. Holding gift cards long-term was like keeping chicken in a plastic kennel in fox country. You might think the kennel well-fenced and the location well-hidden, but eventually one of these damned foxes would get in and go to town, leaving an empty plastic shell when you check next. Keeping the receipts was a form of insurance. If the gift cards were fraudulently drained, then one can still appeal to the gift card issuers to be made whole again, though the process, like insurance, still involved going through more hoops than a basketball at a Wilt Chamberlain game.

After unpacking $10,000 in gift cards and tying them into a neat bundle, I turned to the spreadsheet on the computer. Unfortunately, the credit card offers came at the end of the month when I had already maxed out the $30,000 monthly capacity of the Serve Cards. Fortunately, the *Credit* column indicated that one credit card currently had a balance of $4,000, so I could send the funds non-stop to that card with a Wal-Mart bill pay. The remaining funds would have to be converted into money orders that could deposited into my checking account as a stopover before going back onto the credit cards. Typically, I was loath to go with money orders, but if there's anything I learned as a card smith, it's that opportunity is a lot like time and tide. It may be polite enough to knock, but in the end it waits for no man.

I drove to my go-to Wal-Mart on the Old Road next morning. Pulling into a spot in a mostly deserted parking lot, I performed a quick check of the cards and papers. Stacked into a bundle, the $10,000 in gift cards had the exact same dimensions as a deck of playing cards, though it had a much weightier heft in the hand. The statements for the credit card that I wanted to pay were lying on the passenger seat with the bank name, my name, and a full sixteen-digit account number circled in red ink, and the desired payment amount ($1,998.12) written prominently in the upper right hand corner. Below that was the home mortgage statement. It was almost the end of the month, so I might as well as pay next month's mortgage.

Bristling in the cold morning airs, I power walked the hundreds yards or so between the car and the blue gabled entrance. Passing under the bright iconic yellow starburst logo, I walked into the lobby and breathed a sigh of relief. It was much warmer inside. I glanced at the customer service desk and saw that Glenda helping a customer with returns, as expected. She always worked Sunday to Thursday mornings.

Glenda was the bill pay gatekeeper at this Wal-Mart. A plumpish woman past retirement age, she was always pleasant and helpful, but her taunt face and slightly lopsided posture hinted at the weights on her shoulders. Her eyes had a subdued shine of a gemstone long dulled by weariness, though occasionally in conversations, particularly when talking about her grandchildren, they would glimmer with a hint of lost vivacity. She used to work in finance doing data entry, and she had the amazing ability to type long sequences of digits such as my credit card numbers without looking at the keypad. It was always a wonder to behold; she would hold my credit card statement in one hand, eyes looking directly at the numbers, and on the other hand her fingers would fly across the keypad like a pianist's in the midst of a Beethoven piece. She was very competent, as evidenced by the fact that Wal-Mart let her staff the Service Desk alone five days a week. She must had been quite accomplished in her younger days (she told me she once was an actuary and I believe her), but it seemed that life and circumstances had somehow conspired to force her to toil long into her golden years.

Glenda looked at me and gave a pale smile that failed to disguise the weariness in her eyes. She made a valiant attempt at bantering. "Doing a bill pay this morning?" When I nodded, she quipped, "How did I know that?"

"Because you're my favorite CSR at Wal-Mart." I handed over the credit card statement and Glenda initiated the bill pay process, her hands without looking flying over the terminal as if the keyboard were an extension of her body. I squinted my eyes slightly. The area under her eyes was a shade too dark. "You seem tired this morning. Are you doing okay?"

"It's just my brother. He had some episodes last night, and he was convinced that he needed to see a doctor."

"Did he?"

"We ended up calling the ambulance at one thirty in the morning and they took him to the hospital."

"I'm so sorry, Glenda. Was it something serious?"

"They found nothing wrong with him," she pursed her lips diagonally and gave a shrug. "He was in the army long ago and was never the same afterwards. He's living with me now because he can't handle himself otherwise."

"Did he injure himself in the army?"

She shook her head. "Not physically. He's just a black sheep."

We had reached the payment prompt. Glenda knew from her long experience that I almost always split payments into $500 swipes. The amount displayed was $2,000 even—$1,998.12 for the payment amount and $1.88 for the bill pay fee.

"Split into $500?" she queried.

I nodded assent and we proceeded on the well-choreographed bill pay waltz. I swiped and entered the PIN as she prepped the terminal for the *split payment*, partial payment accepted, the register updated to show the remaining balance reduced by $500, and so on back to the beginning box step.

"So is he still in the hospital?"

"No, he was at the hospital for a couple of hours but then they released him at five thirty this morning. I had to pick him up."

"My goodness! You didn't sleep the whole night, did you?" The bill pay finished and the printer unfeelingly produced the receipt. Glenda reached for the receipt, stapled it to the statement, and handed it back.

"Nope, not a wink. Anything else?"

"Just a money order, please—for one-nine-nine-nine dollars and thirty cents."

I touched her hand briefly. "I know what it's like to have a black sheep in the family. For what it's worth, I think you're a great sister for staying by his side."

Her face lit up with faintest ray of a smile and she punched in the money order information. Once again we engaged in the Wal-Mart waltz.

"You know, at this rate I'll never be able to retire. You'd think that at this age one deserves to sit back and relax. Ride into the sunset sipping Piña Coladas. Or at least sit on rocking chairs and yell at kids to get off your lawn."

"Well, I for one don't want to see you retired," I said and quickly added: "I'd be happy for you if you retired, but I would miss you."

The corners of her lips curved up in a humorless smile. "Don't worry, I can't retire. I need the health insurance—" She broke off and took a few steps to the side where the money order was being printed. Returning and handing it off to me, she continued, "Well, such is life, you know. Anything else?"

"Can you help me pay my mortgage? This time just one payment, no splitting."

I paid for the mortgage with my favorite debit card that offered 5 percent off everywhere Visa was accepted. I wished Glenda good luck and expressed my hope that things would get better. Noticing that a supervisor was coming, I tarried until he was within earshot and then added loudly, "Thanks, Glenda. You're so awesome."

I drove to another Wal-Mart and did another $2,000 bill pay and bought $2,000 worth of money orders before going to work. In the evening I dropped by Wal-Mart and liquidated the last $2,000 of gift card dollars into a money order.

Within the space of two weeks, I had already met the spending requirements on the two Business Gold cards and stashed them in the sock drawer. Through bill pay and money orders, the $10,000 on the gift cards eventually its way back on to the Amex Business Gold, and the 150,000 Membership Rewards points arrived a couple of days after the first month's statement. Total profit, at a conservative estimate, was $1,500, or about a month's worth of work at minimum wage. The fees for the gift cards were $120, and I spent about six hours total on the project: two hours at Ralphs (commuting time included), two hours at Wal-Mart, and another two hours for miscellaneous tasks, including application, activation, money order deposits, and paying off the credit cards.

I kept the 20 drained gift cards in a small plastic bucket, where they shared space with cards that I've emptied within the month. Plenty of things could still go wrong in the few weeks after liquidation. Many greenhorns have learned to their detriment why chucking a card immediately after draining was the most fundamental of taboo in card smithing. Even long after it becomes safe to do so, I don't throw them away. Instead, I toss them into a two-gallon bucket in my garage that contains pretty much every single card that ever went through my hands—one million dollars' worth. It's a secret collecting hobby of mine, modeled after the three-gallon tub in my brother's garage. Whenever I feel down, I run my hand among the jumble of cards, feeling the cool touch of cold plastic as I trawl my fingers along the layers. Truly, very few things in life are more soothing than palming a fistful of plastic cards, say about $50,000 worth, and watching them cascade ungainly downwards between the fingers. It's incredibly therapeutic. Everyone should try it!

THE RIGHT THING TO DO

LET ME TELL YOU ABOUT THE time I had to threaten someone to make them take my money.

I drove into the Wal-Mart parking lot. Smoky billowing clouds completely blanketed the sky horizons to horizons. Dawn was no more than an hour gone, but the dull skies gave no hint of the early hours. Save for a lonely car or two, the parking lot lay empty and desolate. On my passenger seat lay a zip-lock bag containing $3,000 in gift cards A rubber band bound them together lengthwise, while two Serve Cards, my wife's and mine, lay unrestrained and ready to receive the fund infusion. As I glanced at the blue cards I wondered how often actual Serve customers, the ones using the card for its intended purpose, would use the Wal-Mart loading service to deposit several thousand dollars a day like this. Probably as rare as a World Series title for the Chicago Cubs. The Serve Card is designed by American Express as a checking-account alternative to generate profit from the lower segment of the financial market—the so-called "un-banked" or "under-banked"—but it had been co-opted into the beloved tool of choice for card smiths everywhere.

This being a Monday, Glenda staffed the Money Center alone. I waved happily. "Two loads of $1,000 each," I added and soon that amount packed its bags and moved to new residence under my bank accounts.

Walking into the front of the store, I caught a sight that gladdened my heart. Marie was on duty on Register 14. I saw her more often than I saw my best friends, and she is an expert on splitting transactions. No loading instruction ("$800 in four $200 loads," "$700 in two loads, 500 and then 200," etc.) is too crazy or complicated for her blessed hands. She loves to talk to her customers, frequently bantering with regulars, including me, whom she knew by name. When she is on duty, I can liquidate those pesky $200 cards from Staples quicker than frozen lemonade drinks at a Death Valley marathon. She is such a good soul; the only way anyone could be more salt-of-the-earth was to be Lot's wife.

Seeing me coming, her lips curved into the familiar high-wattage smile. "I know what you're here for. Gimme the card."

I handed over my Serve Card and said, "$500, please."

Nothing out of the ordinary happened on the first load. On the second the card terminal flashed the dreaded words *Not Approved,* and the receipt printer spat out a tiny stub the size of a Chinese cookie fortune. *Not approved, error 51,* the (mis)fortune announced.

I glared at the problem card. Damn foxes got into my kennel again.

I ducked into a quiet corner outside the store to assess extend of the damage. A few quick presses on my phone initiated a call to customer service. An automated female voice came on, and I followed her prompt to punch in my sixteen-digit card number along with the CVV code on the back. I then held my breath as the less successful cousin of Siri read my card balance.

"Your current balance is five hundred dollars and zero cents."

Uh . . . what? I scratched my head. Error-51 error generally meant insufficient funds, and yet the $500 remained undisturbed. Weird.

I shrugged it off. It might have been a system glitch, or that I had entered the incorrect PIN. To be sure, I changed the PIN from the automated phone menu and entered Wal-Mart once more.

This time the load proceeded smoothly, and the gift card drained onto the Serve Card as it should.

The drive to work took longer than usual that morning. A multiple car collision had taken place at about the midway point, and traffic inched along for about half a mile upstream and downstream. Outside, the overcast sky seemed different. It had become serene rather than gloomy, though my fellow morning commuters did not share the same thoughts. Car horns every now and then pierced through the morning like audio bubbles breaking from tempers simmering on low.

I leaned back, turned off the radio, and grabbed hold of the drained gift cards in my right hand. Their binding rubber band had been switched lengthwise to indicate the newly drained status. Even though it was physically impossible, the cards felt lighter in the hands. I caressed the empty cards, indulging in the cool touch of plastic against my skin. Ineffable peace radiated from the drained plastic shells. The crawling traffic seemed but a mere crinkle in the order of things. I tapped my fingers contentedly on the steering wheel. There was no need to be angry when there were plenty of reasons to be happy.

Later in the evening, I sat down at my computer to record the day's transaction. The load receipts went into a catalog-size envelope labeled *Load Receipts*, and the drained cards, bundled with the usage-date scribbled on the front, went into a plastic tub. On my spreadsheet, I reduced the count of unused $500 cards by six, and then increased the standing balance on my and Delilah's Serve accounts by $1,500 each. Logging into my Serve account, I bill-paid $1,500 to my Old Blue Cash card. To reflect the transactions on the spreadsheet, I lowered the Serve balance by $1,500 and correspondingly lowered my outstanding debt on the credit card by the same amount.

Something seemed off.

I stared again.

My spreadsheet indicated that I should have $2,700 balance on the Serve, and yet the actual balance indicated $3,200, $500 more than I should have had.

I quickly scanned the last five or six transactions to make sure that everything were in order. No sweating or goose bumps this time, though. Somehow I had ended up with extra money instead of the other way around. If a mistake had to happen, I would much prefer to be on this side of the error.

I located the problem on the first page of transactions. Three transactions had occurred at Wal-Mart in the morning: one deposit of $1,000 and two of $500. Pulling out the load receipts, I did a quick cross-reference of the time stamps. The two receipts I had corresponded to the time stamps of the first and last load from the website. The middle $500 load, however, remained unaccounted for.

Memory of the failed load in the morning came back flying back like a baseball through a window. So that's what happened. Somehow the system had recorded that cancelled load as successful.

The bank had erred in my favor. Proceed past Go and collect $500.

I'd like to say that I didn't think about keeping the money. But that would be false. I didn't keep it, but I thought about it.

After about half an hour of deliberation, I called up Serve customer service. An amicable voice came on, "Hello, this is Charlotte from Virginia. How can I help you today?"

"I would like to report an incorrect load on my Serve Card."

"Sure, I'd be happy to help."

"I loaded $500 today, and my card shows two different $500 deposits."

"I'm sorry to hear that, Mr. Doughsmith. It must be frustrating to have a deposit not show up."

"No, I have the opposite problem."

"Say that again?"

"I'm not missing $500. Serve somehow gave me an extra $500."

There was a pause on the other line. She came back a few seconds later. "You mean you want to report an error of $500 in your favor?"

"Unfortunately, yes." I described the situation in detail and pointed Charlotte to the transaction in question. The phone went silent for a bit as she poked around the system.

"Mr. Doughsmith? The transaction looks entirely normal to me."

"That can't be right . . ."

"Well, I can't remove it because I just can't delete the funds. I could process a refund, if you wish."

"But I don't want the money."

"I can't just delete the money, sir."

"Look, I just want the $500 removed from my account."

"I understand, sir, but in the system the money has to go somewhere. The numbers have to balance. "

"So there's no way for me to return the money?"

"We can't just take money from you, sir."

I chuckled to myself. If I wanted to give American Express money, I'd have to carry a credit card balance like everyone else. "So what do you suggest I do?"

"I recommend that you go back to Wal-Mart and speak with the manager. It is possible that they are missing $500 from this transaction. If that is the case, you can give them $500 and the books would balance."

When the sun rose the next morning I was at Wal-Mart once more. I asked for the manager, and shortly thereafter Kimberly showed up. I had often seen her buzzing about refilling cash registers and handling difficult customers, but I never spoke to her personally. She seemed like she was in a hurry. "Good morning, sir, how may I help you?"

I described my situation. By the time I finished, she no longer seemed like she was in a rush.

"So, you made a load that occurred incorrectly."

"Yes."

"And now you'd like to give the money back?"

"That's right. I think Marie helped me with the load yesterday."

"That's strange. I was here yesterday. Her drawer balanced at the end of her shift."

"So you're not missing any money?"

"No, sir."

"Are you sure?"

"If we're missing $500, we would have known about it yesterday. Let me call someone for a bit."

Kimberly ushered me towards an office in the far end of the store, We entered through a door labeled Employees Only, walking past employees who turned their head curiously in our direction. I felt oddly proud. Probably not many patrons ever get a chance to be in the Employees Only section of Wal-Mart without being forcibly escorted by Loss Prevention or Asset Protection personnel. Even card smiths who move hundreds of thousands per month probably haven't been in the inner sanctum of Temple of Card Smithing. It was underwhelming, though. If you look closely on at the details, you'd see that the doors and hallways were a bit frayed around the edges, as were many of the employees passing to and fro.

Going through a sterile white hallway, we came to a nondescript office in the back. Kimberly introduced me to Mark, the accounting manager. He nodded and firmly shook my hand. "Got a problem, haven't we?" he winked.

Mark made queries on his computer using a program laden with numbers of and symbols. To my layman eyes, the computer screen looked like the green digital rain scene from *The Matrix*. It was probably the accountant version. I twiddled my thumbs as I waited. The constant hum of the air conditioning seemed to drone louder, occasionally punctuated by the Mark's keyboard taps.

He gave an exasperated sigh and turned back to me. "I looked through the records, and I can't find the transaction in question."

"So?"

"It means as far as Wal-Mart is concerned, our books are balanced and we're not missing $500."

"But that money just can't appear about of thin air!"

He shrugged. "Sometimes glitches happen."

"Look, I called Serve and they're not taking responsibility."

"But it's not our problem either, Mr. Doughsmith."

"How about I write a check for $500, and you sort this among yourselves?"

Mark all but shrank back and crossed his index fingers into a crucifix to shield himself. "Oh NO! We can't take your money."

"So what do you suggest I do?"

"I recommend you call Serve again and insist they fix it on their end."

I wanted to pull my hair out. I had $500 on my account, and I just wanted to give it to somebody. American Express or Wal-Mart, I didn't care. They were playing with the responsibility like a hot potato. It was aggravating.

"Let me call Serve customer service. Maybe we'll get somewhere with three-way conference."

After some escalation, I managed to get a hold of Andy from the right department. Mark and I huddled around the phone and attempted anew to square the circle.

Ten minutes later, we had made no progress at all. Andy and Mark continued to insist it was the other side's problem. They tossed accountability back and forth like a dodge ball, evading deftly when it came in flying and then chucking it right back. After some warming-ups, their evasiveness improved, growing to almost Congress-level virtuosity. I strongly considered keeping the $500 and driving home. Considering the frustrating time I'd spent trying to give it back, keeping the money would be a fair compensation. Who knew that it was so difficult to give money to corporations in America?

"Am I clear in understanding that there's nothing you can do?" I asked.

"I don't have any shortage in my books here at Wal-Mart, Mr. Doughsmith."

"And from my end, this $500 is perfectly valid," Andy added.

Mark scratched his head. "Why don't you just give us your phone number and leave it for now?"

"You mean just keep the money and go home?"

"Yes. And if we find where the money is missing we'll call you."

I looked straight at Mark. He couldn't meet my eyes. I got the distinct impression that he was trying to get rid of me or kicking the can to someone else. Wait a minute . . . this sounded suspicious. Was he implicitly bribing me $500 to stop me from trying to give him money? I glanced around the room wondering if I'd by chance stumbled into a Monty Python skit. Maybe just down the hall was the Argument Clinic, and next-door was the being-hit-on-the-head room.

An idea suddenly came. It was worth a try. "You know, I really appreciate both of you for trying to help."

"Our pleasure, Mr Doughsmith."

"But just to cover my butt, can I have a written note? Maybe saying that I tried to return the money but wasn't able to." And to cover both sides, I added: "Also, Andy, can I have an ID number for this conversation?"

Mark and Andy attempted the problem with renewed vigor as if a fire had been lit in their motivation to provide excellent customer service. The name of the game was no longer dodge ball. It had become cooperative basketball, with the two dribbling and passing between themselves as they advanced towards the basket. I leaned back in my chair and let them go at it with obscure technical jargons, feeling like Frodo in *Fellowship of the Ring* when he correctly guessed the password to the Elven-made Doors of Durin. It was *Mellon*, the Sindarin word for friend.

In those days of knights and heroes, the password to open doors was *friend*. Apparently, the modern-day password is *litigation*.

Mark turned to me. "Mr. Doughsmith, I think we found the discrepancy. If you could provide me with $500, I'd be happy to write a receipt."

"And the $500 on my Serve card?"

"That fund would remain there."

That night over dinner, Delilah looked at me with smiling eyes. "So what did you do with the free money from Amex?"

I recounted my trip to Wal-Mart. She put down her fork and touched my hand. "It's the right thing to do."

I sighed. "It's hard to do the right thing in America."

SLEEPLESS IN SEATTLE

DOING THE RIGHT THING IS HARD. Not picking up on the "call of gift cards" is much harder.

I braced myself reflexively, hands gripping the seat divider as the airplane touched the ground. Involuntarily, my stomach muscles tightened into knots for a few brief seconds while shocks reverberated. I had travelled on airplanes enough times to circumnavigate the Earth five times over, but I probably will never get used to the moment when the plane transitions between controlled freefall and coasting on terra firma. Every single jarring jolt was a reminder that our time in the sky is but borrowed time. The flight attendant's voice came on over the slightly crackling speaker system: "Welcome to Seattle."

I looked out the tiny porthole and saw that a slight drizzling rain had dotted the window glass with tiny droplets. Buffeted by the invisible wind, the tiny beads slanted across the window in tiny rivulets. Every now and then, a drop gathered enough weight to streak its way down the window and disappeared below the porthole. Its watery trail soon snapped back into tiny droplets, leaving behind little evidence of its tiny meteoric dart. Seattle was indeed living up to its reputation of prodigious precipitation. It was a welcome sight, coming from Los Angeles, where the weather was so dry that cows were giving evaporated milk. My work had sent me to Seattle for a five-day conference. It would be a break from card cycling, a mini-vacation where I could just focus on work and forget about gift cards.

Shifting in my Economy Plus seat (four extra inches of leg room), I glanced into the back of the cabin where people were shuffling in their seats, antsy to get off the airplane. Behind me an extremely tall young man stood up, head hunched over beneath the overhead bin, and groaned in relief. He was a basketball player at University of Washington, judging by the logo on his sweatshirt and his gargantuan height. At five-foot-nine I was barely comfortable in my Economy Plus seat, and yet this six-foot-five (at least) fella spent the whole flight trussed up like a rotisserie chicken in economy. Poor guy. He tried to tuck his legs under the stowage space of the anterior seat, but to no avail. The laws of physics and the reality of corporate greed simply did not allow it. He spent the entirety of the flight with his knees pressed into the back of the front seat and his feet spilling into the middle walkway. It's a weird justice. The gods had endowed tall people with many advantages in life, but they'd taken it back, with vengeance, when it came to commercial air travel.

I collected my luggage and followed the signs to the car rental counter, where a few minutes in line and a quick chat with a jocular service representative secured a sparkling compact car. In contrast to rental offices I'd seen, this one stood, airport-shop style, in a niche space with no door and the entire entry wall being open to passerby. Seattle seemed to like doing things differently.

"Car insurance?" the representative queried, to which I responded with a head shake. When it came time for payment, I flipped open the wallet and, smiling smugly at how streamlined it was, located my 5 percent cashback card.

After about an hour and a few missed exits later, I drove into the parking lot of my hotel on the outskirt of University of Washington and checked in at the front desk. It was a small boutique hotel nestled in a quiet corner off the main paths near

University of Washington. The walls were decorated in minimalist paintings, and the brightly colored decorations somewhat reminded me of IKEA. When the young blonde clerk asked for a credit card, I slid over the 5 percent PayPal card again, and soon she slid back a receipt. Perusing the charges, I marveled at the earning disparity between my current age of Enlightenment and the previous Dark Age. That morning alone I'd earned $50 cashback while doing no work beyond lifting a few fingers. Back in the college days, it would have taken me almost a week to make that much from my 10-hour-a-week minimum wage job shelving gargantuan tomes in the biomedical library (and that was before Uncle Sam poked his hands in and collected his share).

I opened the door to my room and fell into the blissful embrace of the bed, arms outstretched.

The first night in Seattle, I was perfectly at peace.

When dinner came, I strolled the neighboring University Avenue where all the student-favored (read, cheap) food joints were located. University life hummed vibrantly. Young collegians happily occupied themselves with the demands of youth, their minds still uncontaminated by money. And if my experience in college was any guide, their wallets were uncontaminated by money as well. Dizzying arrays of ethnic foods peppered the side of University Avenue. Laughter and chatter bubbled up from the lively crowd. A smattering of college kids passed by chatting and laughing boisterously. "What a brutal final!" one kid said to general agreement. Another fellow expressed approval: "No kidding. Let's go get wasted." I smiled nostalgically. Student lives never seem to change.

Someone walked by with a grocery bag, and before I knew it, I tracked the plastic bags trying to discern the logo. It was some strange name that I did not recognize. I chuckled at myself. Was I hoping to see the CVS or Rite Aid logo?

A bright neon light beckoned to me like the sight of a lighthouse to a wandering ship. It spelled out *Walgreens* in familiar cursive. The night breeze blew through the air, kicking up the occasional leaves that lay scattered on the sidewalk. One fluttering leaf flew by, cavorting in aerial loops before alighting near the doorstep of Walgreen.

The sight of neatly stacked aisles of grocery, candies, and pharmaceutical products, along with a comforting gift card rack greeted me as I walked through the sliding automatic doors. My eyes narrowed as they adjusted to the bright neon lights. In the late hours of the night, the store stood empty. Empty in a good way, however. Tranquil, undisturbed, and peaceful.

The clerk on duty at the front register perked up from reading her cell phone. She was young, slender, and brunette, doubtless a student at "U-dub."

"Hello! Welcome to Walgreens" came the perky greeting. I nodded and headed straight for the gift card racks, where I found the standard assortments of gift cards broken into the three categories: Use Anywhere, Entertainment, Prepaid Cards. I patted my wallet sadly. In anticipation of a gift card sabbatical, my Old Blue Cash cards remained 1,000 miles away at home in a well-deserved rest. Niggling thoughts tugged on the back of my mind like a kid pulling the sleeves of parents. Should have taken the Old Blue Cash, it said, but I dismissed it summarily. This was a business trip, after all, not a leisure trip.

Reaching for the $500 gift cards, I turned them around in my hands, feeling the soothing glossiness of the packaging against my skin. The money-smithing tracks on the rack were fresh. PayPal reload cards were running low, so cashiers at this store probably have no problem selling on credit. In contrast, the MoneyPak cards on the lower left remained in abundance. Most likely cash-only, just like my own neighborhood. An odd speck of mismatched color behind the Lowe's gift cards caught my eye. These cards were hanging on horizontal metal hooks protruding from the shelf. About midway into the stack, I could see some edges had slightly different hues compared to their neighbors. Sliding a finger to lift up the Lowe's card, I found a payload of PayPal reload cards squirreled therein. Most likely a regular hid them here when they were in abundance, so that they could tide over the out-of-stock periods. Smiling, I let the Lowe's gift cards fall back into place, returning the shelf to its undisturbed condition.

Reconnaissance finished, I walking out the store feeling better. The clerk waved good-bye ("Thank you, come again!") and I waved back. I was no Lone Ranger, but I could read the trail clearly. This was a fairly competitive neighborhood with high turnover. Good thing the regular stores back home were much more generous and much less competitive. There is no place like home, indeed.

On the third night, as I was walking around the neighborhood in search of dinner, my phone chirped. A succinct missive from my brother flashed across the screen: "Promotion at Office Max. $20 off $300 in Visa or MasterCard gift cards. Ends this Sunday." I considered for a few seconds and texted back: "In Seattle now. Taking a break from gift cards until Friday."

Stumbling upon a small gift store, I walked in to search for some small souvenirs. Picking out a trinket for Delilah, I joined the line at the cash register and idly checked the calendar on my phone while waiting for the transaction at the cash register to finish. A short young man, dressed in jeans that had artful holes in certain places designed to evoke coolness through devised carelessness, was having trouble. The elderly cashier had rung up the transaction of about $100 or so, but Ragged Jeans was unable to make his card work.

"Sorry. Every time I swipe the card, there's a screen that pops up asking for my PIN, but I don't know what my PIN is."

"Is it a debit card you're using, sir?"

"I don't know," Ragged Jeans said fidgeting. "I received this card as a gift."

My ears perked up. Professional interest, you see.

"I think there might be a button on the PIN screen that says *Change Payment*," the cashier ventured.

"Yup, I see it."

"If you click on it you can change the payment type to *Credit*."

Ragged Jeans poked at the corresponding button on the screen. "Doesn't work. It flashes a signature screen and then goes back to the payment prompt."

"Do you have another mean of payment, sir?" the cashier queried while casting a jaded eye at the lengthening line. I craned my neck to catch a glimpse the intransigent gift card.

"I don't have enough cash on me." He held up the gift card and peered at it. "I used it the other day at Starbucks and it worked fine . . ."

I caught a glance at the card he was using.

"Excuse me," I stepped in, "I know what the problem is."

They swiveled around, "You do?"

"This purchase is coded to accept either cash or debit transaction only."

"Oo-kay," the cashier enunciated in an obvious tell-me-some-thing-I-don't-know tone.

"Try pressing 0730 for the PIN."

The young fellow stared at the gift card before glaring in my direction. He frowned. Hesitantly, he swiped the gift card, the cashier looking on intently, and punched in the PIN. The machine blinked for a bit. The register printer whirled to life and asthmatically spat out the receipt for the transaction.

Like a pair of marionettes in perfect sync, Ragged Jeans and cashier swiveled in my direction and gawked at me with questioning eyes. Behind me, people in queue remained lost in their own thought, unaware of the financial parlor trick that I just accomplished.

"I work with gift card companies. I'm in the . . . um . . . Loss department."

That satisfied their curiosity, and I continued with my purchase with the now-deferential cashier.

So how did I know the PIN of that gift card?

Elementary, my dear Watson. One glance at the gift card was all I needed. There aren't that many gift card issuers in the money shuffling world, and each issuer has a unique way of setting the default PIN. The cards from Ralphs, for instance, had the default four-digit PIN written in a flap hidden in the back of the packaging. On the other hand, variable-load cards from Vons and Staples use the last four digits of the 16-digit card number as the PIN. The young man was brandishing a card from CVS, which will accept any sequence of 4-digit number for the first debit purchase and then use it as the default PIN thereafter. In all likelihood he'd never used the card for a debit transaction and, consequently, the card would have taken any sequence of four-digit number as the PIN.

But as with many things in life, magic is all about appearances. Suggestion is key. Telling the owner "Just punch in any four-digit sequence" wouldn't be as impressive as saying, "Punch in 0730." Would it?

I tossed restlessly that night.

Thoughts of gift cards gathered in my mind like a pack of squirrel at a bird feeder. Relentless little buggers, they were, scampering away whenever I focused on them, but reassembling whenever I turned my attention to other things, like sleep. I turned in bed. Through the window the sky glowed a luminous black with no hint of star anywhere. The stillness of the night lay unbroken save for the occasional breeze that mutedly rattled trees in the distance. Inside the room only my own breathing disturbed the churning silence. I opened my eyes and stared at the ceiling. Darkness enveloped the room, except for one corner where it was pushed back by my phone's charging light and the dull red display of the hotel alarm clock.

I raised my neck and looked at the clock. It was two in the morning.

I hoisted myself out of the bed and perused the content of my wallet, smiling when I came across the Chase Ink Bold. I'd taken it along because it gave two points back on hotel, plus free rental card insurance if used on a business trip. It also gave five points per dollar at office supplies store.

OfficeMax certainly qualified as an office supplies store.

I fingered the Chase Ink card thoughtfully. Maybe I'd just visit a store or two to check out the promotion. Scope the landscape, you know. It wasn't as if I had anything to do after work anyway, and the special promotion merited an exception to my gift card sabbatical.

I'm sure of it. Without the promotion, I could have resisted the urge. No problem at all.

I drove to OfficeMax after work. It was an OfficeMax on the outskirt of downtown Seattle, nestled in the shadow of a supermarket bustling with activity. Foot traffic, however, did not extend much into the office supply store itself. Above the card rack was taped a sign that was obviously designed in Microsoft Words and printed on a home printer. It advertised the details of the promotion: "Receive $20 instant discount for $300 or more in Visa or MasterCard Gift Card Purchases."

I took five cards to the register and placed them on the conveyor belt in two separate piles. My Chase Ink Bold and driver's license I casually placed on the change counter while scanning the surrounding. My cashier was a young lad, tall, going by the name of Eric and probably not yet able to vote. He had long, lanky limbs that probably still needed some time to fill out. Next to his keyboard was an iPhone lying face-up with the screen being opened to a messaging app. Behind him was the lone other open register.

"Can I get these on two different receipts, please?"

Eric gathered the cards and held one in his long arms. He peered at the cards, unsure about how to proceed. He strained his neck around to the rear register, and said: "Tyler, this guy wants to do two separate gift card transactions. Is that okay?"

Tyler shot me an assessing look, obviously judging to see if I fit the profile of a credit card fraudster. I grinned innocently. He shook his head with finality. "Nope. One transaction on gift cards per customer. Corporate policy."

Interesting. Splitting gift cards into multiple transactions was no-go, but $1,000 in one shot was a-okay. "That is fine with me," I said.

Eric dutifully started peeling the back tab to expose the barcode. One by one, he scanned in the cards and then turned to me, reading the screen: "One thousand thirty-four dollars and seventy cents."

"There's a sign advertising $20 off $300 for gift cards."

Eric looked puzzled. The poor guy was probably new. He huddled with Tyler, and together they pulled out a thick binder from below the terminal register and flipped through the pages like a bunch of magic apprentices looking through the master's spell book. Eventually they found the promotional barcode, which they scanned into Eric's register. Instantly, the balance due updated to display $974.75 instead of $1,034.75. Tyler crossed the few steps back to his register, and Eric sneaked a glance at his phone screen while waiting for me to finish paying.

I walked out of OfficeMax elated. One thousand dollars in gift cards only cost me $975, and that's before factoring in the 5 percent cashback.

I blinked.

Whoa . . . $975?

Scrambling, I took out the receipt and scrutinized the writings. No wonder the amount seemed so low. At the very bottom before the totals was the line *Discount—$60*. Instead of the expected $20 instant rebate, OfficeMax had given $60!

I furrowed my brow as I scanned the rest of the receipt for clues, but the stubborn paper offered none. It looked like every other office supplies receipt I'd purchased, except for the one terse line detailing the discount. Fingering the cards, I wondered if the error was repeatable. In this gift card business, the boundary between a fluke and an opportunity was more like the Rome-Vatican border rather than, say, the US-Mexico border. The purchase amount of $1,000, however, hinted at one possible explanation. It was possible that OfficeMax programmers had coded the registers to give a $20 discount for *every* $300 and allowing for multiple bonuses within the same transaction. I shook my head warily. Such a big corporation couldn't possibly make that elementary mistake, could it?

To test the hypothesis, I drove to another OfficeMax. Though the car navigation software indicated that the closest one was fifteen minutes away, it seemed like fifty miles. Once parked, I made a beeline for the gift rack from my car so fast that a rear observer would have seen my image red-shifted. Here too the sign advertising the promotion was taped to the rack, and plenty of cards were in stocks. Apparently the card smith onslaught had yet to take its toll. I took six cards to the register. If my hypothesis was correct, $1,200 in gift cards should produce $80 in discount when the promotional barcode was applied.

The transaction at the register proceeded much faster than the last one. I pointed the clerk to where the coupon code was stored in the "promotional coupons folder." "Look for the week of June 9th," I suggested. He found and applied the code without trouble. After the promotional code was scanned, the total balance dropped from $1,241.70 to $1,161.70.

Bingo! My hypothesis was correct.

The discount was indeed for $20 for every $300. It was lucrative to be right. Someone at the IT department of OfficeMax would have some serious explaining to do later.

I stole a glance at the clerk to see if he had noticed the hugely profitable discrepancy. He was a young and looked like the students I saw on the University Avenue; most likely he was a part-timer while going to the university. He had not noticed, and most likely didn't care about OfficeMax's loss or gain. While I swiped my cards, he stared idly out the window with distant eyes.

I walked out the store wearing the same grin that was on Ali Baba's face when he discovered the passage to the treasure cave. When I left the hotel that morning, I had merely hoped to assuage the gift card hankering, but I stumbled into a veritable gold mine. While I still felt guilty for giving in to the temptation of gift cards, part of me was glad that I had succumbed. If promotions were hotels, the deal as I first heard it was at best a Motel 6, but in truth it was closer to a Four Seasons.

I glanced at my watch. Even though the sun still hovered high above the horizon with its beams still bright and strong, the clock indicated that it was seven o'clock at night. Winding the plastic bags around the gift cards, I considered calling it a day and return to the comfort of the hotel. The day had been long. I worked nine-to-five and didn't even have dinner, having only grabbed a quick snack on the way to the car. The profits were en route to my bank accounts, and the gift cards could be liquidated at leisure once back home. There was nothing left to do in Seattle that could not wait for California. Dinner would have been great at that moment!

I picked up the phone and, exhaling a long resigned breath, instructed the virtual assistant to "Navigate to the nearest Wal-Mart."

In the lateness of the hour Wal-Mart was not surprisingly buzzing with foot traffic. Normally I tried to avoid these hours because the resulting demographics and activities always resembled the Tatooine bar scene from *Star Wars*, but I needed to get my fix. The customer service counter was packed, and likewise the check-line lanes had lines stringing for tens of minutes. Fortunately Kate, the ATM kiosk, stood blessedly deserted in the Money Center. Plugging a pair of earphones into the machine to silence the indiscreet automatic voice, I "fed the birds." Around me, the hustle and bustle of the teaming masses continued, oblivious to the thousands of dollars flowing in this discreet corner.

Within the space of fifteen minutes, all 11 gift cards were drained. On the way out I grabbed a PowerBar for dinner. I walked out the store munching on the bar and feeling like a character in *Ocean's Eleven* when the gang strolled outside of the Bellagio after their heist. The sun had already dipped below the horizons, and now the lights of the city were taking turn sparkling beneath a beaming moon. Taking a deep breath, I savored the coolness of the night air before exhaling contentedly. I missed the feeling. Of all the parts in cycling money, I loved best walking out of Wal-Mart after an error-free card run, empty cards in hands and peace upon mind. I strolled back to the car in contentment. You know movie scenes where the heroes walk swaggeringly in slow-motion *Reservoir Dogs* style? It felt just like it.

Back in the comfort of the hotel, I dialed Delilah, "So, you have any plans for the weekend?"

"Aw, you want to go on a date?"

"Um . . . yes?" I ventured tentatively.

"Wait a minute. I know that voice."

"You do?"

"You want me to go buy gift cards with you this weekend, right?"

"Okay, you got me." Nothing got past the wife. "But this is some good money."

"How good?"

I recounted the details of the programming error. She went silent for a bit, and in the silence I could visualize her wrinkling her eyebrows. "Wait a minute . . . something's off."

"There is?"

"How's this different from the time Amex gave you $500? You gave that money back and now you want to take advantage of this coding error."

"That's simple. The Amex money was unearned."

"Hmm . . . I don't know about that."

"Remember the time United Airlines mistakenly listed a round-trip to New York for $10 and we were rushing to buy it?"

"Yeah . . . ?"

"Same idea. It's all fair game if you gotta go earn it."

"Okay, so what's your plan?"

"I want to hit four OfficeMax stores. Between you and me, we could make $200 per store."

"You make it sound like we're going to commit armed robbery!"

"This isn't armed robbery. It's more profitable." I sweetened the pot. "We could go to Korean BBQ on Saturday. OfficeMax's treating."

She breathed a sign of resignation long-suffering spouses of card smiths everywhere knew only too well. "Fine, I'll go."

Stacking the used cards into a stack and binding them with a rubber band, I thought about my trip. It was clear I needed to be honest with myself. The business trip was supposed to be a mini-sabbatical from manufactured spending, but the vacation had turned out to be more of a forced exile. I had managed to convince myself the trips to OfficeMax were justified in light of the gift card promotion and that I could perfectly resist the siren call of the cards otherwise. But the trip to Wal-Mart afterwards (without dinner no less) completely stripped away the fig leaf.

I sighed in defeat. Without realizing it, I was in deep. If obsession was the enemy, then Seattle was my Waterloo. I like to call the Game my hobby, but really it was just a hobby in the same manner that Josephine was just Napoleon's female friend.

SECOND HONEYMOON

AS PROMISED, I TOOK DELILAH TO Europe for another honeymoon to Europe, courtesy of 120,000 American Airline miles. The trip was three weeks long, but Seattle had taught me how to deal with the gift card itch. Temptation is a lot like health care: an ounce of prevention is worth a pound of cure. The key is never to carry credit cards on a vacation. Without any means of buying gift cards, I was totally immune to temptation.

The hubbub of the airport droned on as I angled a water bottle into the stream of water arching from the public water fountain and watched as the water level rose steadily. Behind me I could hear the incessant whirl of luggage wheels passing back and forth while the overhead airport public announcement system mumbled unintelligibly. The upcoming trans-Atlantic direct flight to Berlin was about 11 hours in duration, and I aimed to have plenty of my secret weapons against jetlag: hydration (check) and melatonin (check). It's always a good idea to start a vacation on the right foot.

I tossed the bottle to Delilah when I returned to the gate. We each had one backpack and one standard-sized suit case, wherein we had packed enough essentials to last three weeks. I had watched her pack her luggage earlier, and I could have sworn that in her magical hands the fabric of space seemed to stretch and unfurl within the confines of the bag, making the inside deceptively larger than what it seemed from its outward appearance. Materials that would have taken me three pieces of luggage were effortlessly charmed to fit snugly together within one. It was a good thing, though, considering the sprawling itinerary in store. Our three-week itinerary included flying straight into Berlin, and then flying home from Lisbon. From Berlin, the plan was to visit the canals of Amsterdam and the romance-drenched streets of Paris, before flying to the Iberian peninsula and passing the remaining time between Gaudi-inspired Barcelona, tapas-laden Madrid, and tram-lined Lisbon.

I stared outside the airport glass windows. The busing airplanes came and went in the early afternoon, each forming an invisible line connecting it to its destination and all terminals on its path. How long would it take before the tracing line connects back onto this destination, I wondered. Perhaps it was the fate of airplanes to travel the sky forever and never have a place to call home. A poor fate indeed.

In a way, the money smithing business is like an airport. Every time a gift card is purchased, the corresponding funds take off into the freedom of the world, from whence it travels to destinations far and wide before eventually returning to the originating credit card. The manufactured spender is command control, striving to keep the optimum balance of putting as many planes in the air as possible per month within the limited available runways while avoiding accidents . . .

"Something on your mind?" Delilah queried between sips of water.

"Just missing home."

"Already?"

I pinched my index finger about half an inch away from the thumb. "Only a tiny bit."

"We'll be back in no time. If it's like last trip, three weeks will be over in a blink of an eye."

"I already miss my grocery stores," I said, wrinkling my brows dolefully.

"They'll probably miss you too, considering the lost revenue."

Twelve hours later, we arrived in Berlin, where we filed into a shuttle that rambled from the airport to downtown, passing the famous Bundestag and the historic Unter den Linden before stopping at the final destination near the Fernsehturm—the iconic radio tower that stood soaring above the skyline of historic Berlin.

Surprisingly, Berlin turned out to be one of my favorite European cities. It was less touristy and more affordable than either London or Rome, and much more photographic than I expected, especially at night. By accident on the third night we stumbled onto an Oktoberfest celebration near the train station at Alexanderplatz. Much smaller in scale compared to the Bacchanalian celebration in Munich, the celebration nevertheless harkened to the festive Bavarian sensibilities. Wooden village houses shared the square with makeshift windmills and carnival games where children excitedly play under the watchful eyes of parents. Waitresses dressed in the traditional dirndl buzzed back and forth like bees, carrying large steins of beer and plates of chicken and pork knuckles. In the distance the radio tower stood silently against the starless night sky. Delilah and I shared a large stein of beer and some victuals inside an alpine style wooden beer house. In the lateness of the night surrounded by glimmering carnival lights and a rowdy German crowd drowning beer after beer in raucous conversation, we caught a glimpse into the German way of life. It explained a lot of the differences between the straitlaced northern European and their easy-going southern neighbors. The Italians may have *la dolce vita*—the sweet life— year-round, but the Germans seem content to compress a year's worth of revelry and excess in the space of Oktoberfest.

Leaving Berlin, we arrived in Amsterdam after an eight-hour train ride, a mind-numbingly exhausting trip of mostly identical pastoral scenery occasionally broken by small villages and cities. The first sights that greeted us outside the train stations were a multitudinous number of bikes and the ubiquitous canals. It seemed that one could not walk fifty feet in any direction without seeing bikes or canals. It is said that Amsterdam is the Venice of the North, a reputation well-deserved. However, we specifically chose Amsterdam for its other reputation as the Colorado of Europe.

The first night, we walked down the Red Light District, where numerous shopping-sized red-fringed windows gave a view into the Netherlands' liberalism. Passersby—mostly tourists, it seemed—stood gawking outside the windows while young attractive women in scant lingerie posed like models at the end of a catwalk. Each parlor was lit by the eponymous red light, basking the contents of the room and the women in a rich scarlet hue that evoked vague associations of sordidness and seediness. Every so often, a nervous laugh or giggle could be heard among the droning whispers.

A few hundred yards off the main canal, we came across a gaggle of young men, each likely no older than twenty. One, seemingly the gang leader, knocked on a window in which an attractive blonde lady stood. She poked her head outside a small door to the right, and they engaged in negotiation. "Fifty euros for 15 minutes," she said. The lad pointed at a fresh-faced comrade in the back and gestured for a reduced rate. Her lips curved up into a bemused smile at the sight of Fresh Face but he avoided her gaze. Eventually she relented and the remaining boys, except for Fresh Face, cheered. A collection was taken up and each lad chipped into a pot that was remitted ceremoniously to the hands of the lingerie-clad lady. She beckoned him to come, and the lucky fellow, flanked on either side by a companion to prevent cold feet, walked up to the window and disappeared inside. His companions lounged outside, some leaning against the wall, and waited for his return.

I grinned at Delilah and said, "Lucky lad."

"Why? Because he's getting lucky tonight?"

"No, because he's got some great friends."

We devoted the last day in Amsterdam to its other specialty—"coffee shops." It was a day that we both remember fondly if somewhat hazily. We scheduled no museum, landmark, or restaurant of any kind. In the morning, I made a jaunt over to the nearest coffee shop to get some advice on their "products," and the rest of the day passed by in a blur of hilarity and munchies. By the time we left Amsterdam, it was our new all-time favorite city.

Paris lived up to its reputation as la Ville Lumière—the City of Lights. The weather had been pleasant so far, but by the time we arrived in Paris, the skies had filled with dark clouds. On the first evening, we picnicked on the fountain banks in Jardins du Trocadéro under the shadow of the Eiffel Tower. Crowds of tourists thinned as the evening sun dipped across the horizon. It was what photographers called the golden hour, the period of time shortly before and after dawn and dusk when daylight is softer and richer in red tones. After the sun set, we were treated on the hour to a light show that lit up the entire Eiffel Tower in a dazzling, sparkling light for five whole minutes. A brief shower followed the sunset, covering the city in a skin of reflective water. While everyone else made haste to avoid the rain, we huddled under our umbrella and were rewarded with the most magical atmosphere after the rain departed. The lights, now shining in a mostly deserted park, played merrily in the rain puddles and glistening buildings, and above us the Eiffel Tower traced an arc in the sky with its lighthouse style beacon. Everything seemed more intimate as the accidental rain washed away the incessant city buzz, and we resolved from then on to come out after night rain whenever possible. (If you ever happen to be near La Grand Place in Brussels after a night rain, do yourself a favor and stroll out with your camera. You won't regret it.)

On the second day, we visited the Sacré-Cœur Basilica, the travertine church at the summit of Montmartre, the highest point in the city. An inclined esplanade cascaded downward from the terrace, a stairway flanking both sides. On the left a funicular provided easy lift to those reluctant to brave the steps, and in the middle tourists and locals alike mingled in the grassy expanse. Some lounged in the sun, some read, tourists took selfies, and locals basked in the *joie de vivre*. Delilah and I stood on the edge of the terrace overlooking the grassy hillside observing the crowd below. "Lots of scams going on here," she observed.

A few young women were walking about with clipboards plying the familiar sign-against-drug scam. It was the same scam we'd seen in Italy. Once signed, the scammers would demand a donation and, upon being rejected, would point to fine print on the clipboard. "Minimum 10 Euro required," it probably said. Others, mostly swarthy young men of foreign nationalities, worked the Paris string scam. They attempted to engage in innocent conversation, and at some point ambushed tourists by encircling the wrist or fingers with colored strings or make-shift bracelets. The bracelets were designed with an obscure latching mechanism, making it difficult for the surprised tourist to remove at a moment's notice. The scammer would then demand payment for the string or bracelet and, if not satisfied, doggedly follow and harass the tourist until money exchanged hands.

A ruckus drew my attention to the right side near the midway point of the funicular, where an American tourist seemed to be distraught. The security of her purse seemed to have been compromised and contents were stolen. Clutching her purse, she frantically scanned the ground and the crowd for either the lost contents or the culprits. Her husband stood helpless nearby. A few kind-hearted bystanders offered consolation; others walked straight on while stealing a pat or two on their pockets or wallets to ensure they were still there.

"Did you secure everything?" Delilah asked.

"Everything's still here," I patted my money belt where passports and credit cards were stowed. "It'd take an exceptionally smooth pickpocket to remove them."

"Camera?"

"In my jacket. Zipper pulled up. No worries."

"Take good care of them."

On the second-to-last night, we went out after sunset to do night photography along Pont Alexandre III and the Petit Palais. Scintillating light lit up the Seine River as it flowed calmly along the bank where couples sat murmuring and musicians coaxed melodies from willing instruments. Off in the distance, the Eiffel Tower stood high above the skyline. Occasionally a tourist boat ambled under the bridge and drenched the entire bank in bright neon-blue lights. The shimmering lights of the city met the edge of the river where it became pliant and danced along with the ebb and flow of the waves.

We spent two hours capturing the magic of the soft city light. To celebrate a productive night, we resolved to treat ourselves to mojitos in a bar next to our hotel near Gare du

Nord. It was situated on Rue du Faubourg-Saint-Denis, a working-class street that saw very little tourist activities. Though located barely a mile from the Louvre in the heartland of France, the atmosphere seemed to have been transported from the southern coast of France. Ethic restaurants, bakeries, and computer accessory shops lined the sides of the thoroughfare. Halfway between hotel and the subway station was a restaurant that sold the most beautifully buttery roasted potatoes. In the front window three rotisserie skewers with their poultry fares rotated leisurely. A tray under the chickens contained peeled *pomme de terre*, which were continually basted with the drippings. The potatoes were good enough to snack on or serve as an entire meal. It was unpretentious but by no means unsophisticated, and unsurprisingly, it turned out to be one of the things we missed most about France.

Making our way past the roasted chicken and potato restaurant among the teeming mass of night walkers, I accidentally brushed my hand against my jacket pocket. Something seemed off, something like a nagging feeling in the back of the brain waving for attention from the consciousness.

I quickly patted my jacket pockets and broke out in cold sweat. It was empty. I was positive that the camera was tucked therein, but no amount of searching or wishful thinking could now produce it. The pocket lay completely flaccid with the zippers wide open.

I stopped dead in the road. Delilah turned around and caught the frantic look in my eyes. "What's the matter?"

"The camera is gone."

Her eyes widened. "Calm down. Check your wallets and passport first."

I checked. Money and identification documents were still in order. The camera, our only one, was definitely gone, and a whole evening of night photography lost, with half the honeymoon still to come.

I sighed and met Delilah's eyes, bracing myself for rebuke or an I-told-you-so. I deserved it, and I would have absolutely done so in her shoes.

None came.

She gave me a bracing hug. "Let's get those mojitos."

The celebratory drinks turned out to be analgesic. Delilah was determined not to let the loss of the camera ruin the trip. "We'll just go through the remaining trip with cell phone cameras," she said. Brave words, I knew. She probably loved photography as much as one could love anything without marrying it.

We didn't have to resort (God forbid!) to the cell phone cameras. The next morning, we made our way to the electronic store, Darty, the Best Buy of France, and bought a replacement camera. In the evening we returned to Pont Alexandre and reproduced the night photography session. The dancing lights and glowing sky were unchanged from the previous evening, but different water flowed under the bridge. Though a few hundred euros poorer, I had learned a bit more about my wife and myself and was the richer for it.

The occasionally cloudy weather in Paris gave way to intense sun in Barcelona. Now that we were in southern Europe, the prosperous clean appearance gave way to controlled chaos and a slightly tattered general atmosphere. Time, however, seemed to flow along at an unhurried pace.

We spent most of our time in Barcelona tracing the architectural legacy of Antoni Gaudi, assisted daily by generous servings of sangria. For me, the stay in the capital city of Catalonia was especially memorable because it included October 12, 2014—a day that would forever live in infamy among the manufactured spending community. Amazon had decreed the date as one on which the Amazon Payment, much beloved of the credit card smiths, was to be shuttered forever. For three years the service had stood as the Holy Grail of money shuffling, allowing subscribers everywhere to send money from credit cards to friends and spouses free of charge. Points, cashback, and miles flowed freely. Alas, it was not to last. The news had rocked the community when it came out one month prior, and by the time October came around most people had already graduated from anger, denial, sadness, and bargaining to resigned acceptance.

When the fateful date rolled around, the online forum dedicated to Amazon Payment surged with activity. It was a vigil. People from all walks of life whose lives had been touched and benefited by Amazon Payment came to pay their respects. A diverse lot hailing from all parts of the country, our lives were disparate threads in the grand garment destiny but tied together through the one common thread that was Amazon Payment. We exchanged fond stories of the soon-to-depart old friend, shared war stories, reminisced about the glory days, and consoled each other about the dark uncertain days ahead.

For a long time Amazon Payment was my go-to option for easy spending, and afterwards it often came to my aid when I had a gift card gone awry that needed urgent liquidation. The airfare for my first honeymoon was funded exclusively through its Send Money feature, and I owed much of my career as a card smith to the memories of that trip. Amazon Payment's largesse came out on paper to be thousands of dollars per year and potentially millions of miles, but it was also a close friend whose worth cannot be measured in numbers. Who can put a numerical value on the laughter of a lazy evening or friendships forged in impromptu dinners halfway across the world? What is the measure of memories spent catching drops of sunshine and dancing to the song of changes? In the financial history of the world from the first moment that the Sumerians invented clay currency until these modern days of digital economy, there was no financial service so beloved; and there probably will be no service like it until the end times.

When the clock struck midnight, I felt great turmoil in the Force as the anguish of a million card smiths reverberated through space. And just like that, Amazon Payment slipped the surly bonds of this world and passed into memory.

Other than the sad passing of our dear "friend," we loved Barcelona. Our room was on the third floor with a balcony overlooking Portal de l'Àngel, a large shopping thoroughfare that extends from Avinguda Diagonal to the Gothic Quarters. A pedestrian-only zone, it was one of the most visited streets, lined on both sides with the likes of Gucci and Versace, and busy year-around with locals and tourists alike. In the evening, the pulsing street traffic slowed down to a crawl as tourists retreated to their leased domiciles while the locals shifted towards more gustatory nightlife centers.

On the last night in Barcelona, we sat outside the balcony enjoying the night air with sangria in hand. Blessedly cool night breezes replaced the sweltering heat of the day. It was almost eleven o'clock at night, and traffic below had reduced to an occasional straggling pedestrian.

A truck drove onto the street and stopped right below our balcony. It was the size of a moving van, but the top of the cargo box was open. From our elevated vantage point we could see into the box where discarded cardboards lay jumbled into wavy heaps. Three men in grime-stained overalls descended from the truck. One of them, an older gentlemen with a portly frame, greeted a shop owner amicably, and shortly afterwards the three started loading empty and compacted cardboard boxes from the clothing shop.

The blare of a police siren interrupted the tranquility of the night. A car pulled up and out came a youthful though officious policeman. He demanded to talk to the older gentleman, whereupon the two engaged in a heated exchange. I didn't understand Catalonian beyond the obligatory *hola* and *gràcies*, but the officer seemed to be asking for documentation or a permit that the older gentlemen didn't have. A few curious passersby stopped to watch. The older gentleman became increasing agitated, and his tall friend joined in the remonstration. The officer seemed to be sympathetic, but he repeatedly tapped on his notebook. "Rules are rules," he seemed to insist.

The last of the three workers, a wiry fellow, leaned against the truck and lit up a cigarette. His two companions remained locked in argument with the policeman, but the young man was resigned to its futility. His face appeared no older than twenty-five, yet the slump of his posture seemed to carry the weight of decades. He sagged his head against the truck and gazed into sky, which glowed luminously in blessed isolation from the demands of life. The skyward reflection of city light blocked out most stars, and the few that managed to shine through were dim. Occasionally the young fellow blew out long wisps of smoke that immediately were caught and buffeted into oblivion by the unfeeling night breeze.

It was a haunting image that I haven't been able to forget— an image of a striving spirit crushed under the weight of implacable institutions. I turned to look at Delilah, and in her pensive eyes I knew she was thinking of the porter we'd seen in Venice during the first honeymoon. As the bard said, "All the world's a stage." Here thousands of miles away in a different time and culture, the same unfortunate play was taking place. Different actors and different backdrop, but the theme of downtrodden lives remained the same. Sometimes life is a lot harder than it needs to be.

At the end, the young officer wrote a ticket and left without ceremony. The three workers, much crestfallen, packed up their truck, slamming the door as it closed. They drove off into the glittery lights of Portal de l'Àngel and eventually disappeared into the darkness.

Lisbon was easily the most affordable city of the entire trip. As part of the PIIGS (Portugal, Italy, Ireland, Greece, and Spain) countries that were in serious sovereign financial troubles, Lisbon was laboring under the weight of austerity. It was evident in the depressed local prices. Hotels could be had for a third the price of its equivalent in France, while food was easily twice or trice cheaper. Our hotel was located on a small road just a bit north of the popular local meeting place, Rossio Square. It bordered a cobblestoned road flanked by innumerable restaurants, each of which apparently had a hawker who stood in the street striving to make customers of passersby. Amazingly persistent, they shot around conversation starters with abandon: "Where are you from?" "Can I show you the menu?" "Only local seafood here." Every journey we took between the hotel and Rossio Square during dining hours was like running a gauntlet, until we wised up and took a small back road that cut through most of the advertising onslaught.

On the first evening, as was the wont in every new city, Delilah and I set out to find a place to dine. She took the lead.

We walked down the main road braving hawking overtures with stony faces. She passed through proffered menus and claims of authentic Portuguese cuisine like a woman on a mission. I followed suit, knowing better than to interfere. In every city so far she had displayed an uncanny knack for locating great local diners. Time and time again she found *trattorias* and holes-in-the-wall whose quality and tastiness far surpassed what their humble appearance suggested. It was a skill that was beyond my ken, but I've made peace with the fact that, as the bard once said, "there are more things on heaven and earth . . . than are dreamt of in [my] philosophies." Delilah can probably tap into the gourmet vibes that emanate like electro-magnetic fields from great restaurants, and she followed the gradient lines like a gustatory Geiger counter.

She stopped by a small intersection and looked to either side. "This way," she said, pointing into a mostly empty alley. The few people that walked about seemed to be local. About a hundred feet down she paused by a restaurant with a small glass window displaying a variety of fresh fish on a bed of ice. There was a small crowd of elderly locals waiting outside. "This one," she declared.

The locals were apparently there for the weekly special, which appeared to be some sort of stew that prominently featured a pig foot. Every table had the weekly special, but we opted for the grilled fish. Our waiter was a chubby working-class bespectacled fellow named Abilio, who probably knew no more than 30 words in English. Our Portuguese was worse than his English, but we managed to communicate just fine if somewhat inefficiently via gestures. Delilah pulled him outside and pointed at a pompano-like fish and a piece of salmon within the display window. Within about 15 minutes two plates of perfectly-grilled fish appeared on our table, accompanied by a simple side salad with oil-and-vinegar dressing and a serving of potatoes so buttery that they were easily on par with the dripping-roasted *pomme de terre* we had in France. Half a liter of house red wine rounded out the meal. Simple, unpretentious, and mouthwateringly tasty.

We came back often, and soon became friends with Abilio. We signed to him that we considered his restaurant among the gustatory highlights of the trip, to which he replied with a simple "Obrigado" and an appreciative nod.

On the last night in Europe, we celebrated the bittersweet ending in his restaurant. We ordered the fish that we liked best.

"Half liter?" Abilio inquired of alcohol accompaniment.

I nodded but quickly changed my mind. "What the hell. Make it a full liter."

The next hour passed by in pleasant reminiscence. The three weeks had indeed gone by in a blink. Deducting credit card discounts, our bank accounts were $5,000 poorer, but our lives were much richer for it. There was once a time in my life when I considered $5,000 for a three-week trip a profligate waste of money, but sitting there in Lisbon gazing into my wife's eyes I realized that it was a phenomenal bargain, even more so when Chase, American Express, and Capitol One were paying the bill. Travel had a way of bringing out the best and worst of people. The unfamiliar environment and shifting cultural norms tend to pull people out of their comfort zones, stripping away the veneer of civility that habitually mask the true personalities—good and bad. There probably are few better tests of a relationship than exhaustion, being out of one's elements, and discomfort—all of which are in plentiful supply when venturing far from the safety and routines of home. Travel is the crucible in which strong relationships burnish while weaker ones wither. When our son comes of age, I'll definitely advise him to travel with his beloved before marriage. It's a good way to separate the wheat from the chaff.

I told Delilah my travel-before-marriage principle. Wings before rings, I called it. She nodded with lips pursed. "Good advice. I wish someone told me that when I was young."

"Why? Would I not pass the test?"

She laughed with a twinkle in her eyes.

I leaned back and closed my eyes to savor the unhurried evening.

"I got an idea," she said.

I opened my eyes. "Shoot."

"Let's go on another honeymoon."

"Sure, where?"

"How about Istanbul, Athens, and Munich?"

Long ago my knee-jerk reaction would have been to channel Ebenezer Scrooge's bah humbug response. Now I just smiled with a calm shared only by travel hackers and the top 1 percent. It was the kind of smile that said, "Money and distance are no object."

"As you wish."

We gave a generous tip. The world started spinning slightly as the one liter of wine started kicking in.

"We should complement the chef on his fantastic dishes," Delilah whispered.

"Good idea! Let me get Abilio."

"No need. I can see the chef from the window."

Before I got a chance to protest, she jumped up and within a few seconds stood before the glass window. I saw her give three quick impetuous taps on the glass. The chef stopped grilling fish and looked up.

Delilah gave the double thumbs-up gesture.

I caught up to her. The chef looked her dumbfounded and turned to me with questioning eyes. I pointed at the wife and then pointed an index finger at my forehead and made a circular motion.

He snickered and waved back. And that was how we ended our second honeymoon.

Less than 24 hours later, we were back in America battling jetlag and trip nostalgia. Less than 72 hours later, the sun rising over California found me at Ralphs. It was a fine morning to be home and a great morning to buy gift cards. I placed four cards in two separate piles on the conveyor belt. In the early morning the registers were completely empty except for one cashier. I waved hello to Jeff the young supervisor as he walked by.

"Good to see you again," he said. "We haven't seen you for weeks."

"Good to be back. I didn't think you'd notice my absence."

"Accounting told me gift card revenues fell of the cliff last month." He winked. "I figured it was you."

AIRLINE MILES BASICS

I'M NOT A PROFESSIONAL TRAVEL HACKER. My specialty in this field in cashback, but I've earned more than one million airline miles and redeemed close to that number on various domestic and international itineraries. That's about enough to grasp the basics of the airline miles game and to figure out the answer to that question I had long ago in Florence: "Who's paying for all this?" Let me tell you about the greatest money-raking scheme of the twentieth century. It's called frequent flyer programs. And no, it's not the typical consumers who do the raking.

Frequent flyer programs first started in 1981 when American Airlines introduced AAdvantage. The purpose was to reward customers for flying—every customer received a mile for every mile traveled. The mile balance could be redeemed for future flights, essentially amounting to a rebate. Since most flights tend to have unsold seats (about 10 percent on average, I believe), it cost the airline very little to give customers Monopoly money, I mean *frequent flyer miles*, that they could later use to redeem for seats that would have gone unsold. A round trip to the East Coast from Los Angeles, for instance, would have produced about 5,000 frequent flyer miles while a trip from New York to Rome would have earned about 8,500 miles. American Airlines also added car rentals and hotel stays to the program, enabling travelers to earn AAdvantage miles by using a membership number when booking affiliated services. The miles could only be redeemed through American

Airlines, starting at a rate of 25,000 miles for a round-trip flight anywhere within the continental United States.

Reception to the frequent flyer program was a huge success. Not surprising, people loved getting loyalty points on trips they would have taken anyway. It was a win-win situation. The airlines gave away unsold seats, thereby earning a huge amount of goodwill and customer loyalty at nominal cost. The customers, on the other hand, received a rebate on their bookings that ranged between 5 percent and 20 percent, depending on the itinerary. Not to be left at a competitive disadvantage, United Airlines started its MileagePlus program and even offered an enrollment bonus of 5,000 miles. The remaining major airlines soon followed suit with their own frequent flyer program implementations.

In the years since their inception, frequent flyer programs have evolved to include many venues for earning miles. The focus, unfortunately, shifted from promoting loyalty to profit generation. The original scheme of earning frequent flyer miles for actual distance travel remained, though most airlines have switched from a distance-based scheme to a revenue-based scheme. That is, airline miles are no longer given based on distance traveled, but rather on a multiplicative factor (ranging from five to 10 times the amount paid). Ranked by popularity, the earning method of choice (by a mile) for most people is the time-tested credit card application, which usually offers between 30,000 and 50,000 miles each. Through expanded networks, however, it is now easier than ever to earn airline miles through affiliate services. A non-exhaustive list, for instance, includes the following: buying web services; buying, selling, or refinancing properties; making between $15,000 and $100,000 deposits to Fidelity brokerage accounts; signing up for television programs; paying utility bills; opening checking accounts or maintaining a balance at Bank Direct (60,000 miles per year for a $50,000 balance); making purchases on airline-affiliated credit cards or debit cards; paying for dinners with credit cards that are enrolled in an affiliated dining program; using an online shopping portal that offers between three and 10 miles per dollar spent; taking a survey, getting a home security system, or donating to a charity.

Although the venues for earning miles have exploded in the last few decades, the number of seats available for award redemption has, at best, only kept pace with carrier's routes. A reasonable figure I've seen is that between 5 and 10 percent of each flight are *award seats*; the rest are called *revenue seats*, for obvious reasons. While the number of routes has grown linearly in the past few decades in accordance to population growth, the number of people accumulating frequent flyer miles has grown exponentially. Talk with any airline mile enthusiast about the past, and a leitmotif emerges about the declining value of the miles. It's simple supply and demand. Just a decade ago when the art of earning miles was still fairly esoteric, there were fewer people who commanded the knowledge and earned the stash necessary to redeem for free travel. Because travelling free of charge back then was relatively painless, the miles had more value. Back in 2000 when David Phillips earned 1.25 million miles from puddings, the miles were easily worth two cents each. Nowadays with the higher difficulty of redeeming an award seat and the numerous surcharges, I would say that they are probably worth one cent each on average, if that.

Compounding the general low availability, airline miles have many features detrimental to general consumer interest. How do they fleece customers? Let me count the ways. Airline miles, with few exceptions, typically expire between 12 and 36 months from the date of last activity. This certainly constitutes a tax on lack of activity, though punitive seizure is perhaps a more appropriate label. Even when redemption is successful, airlines still try to nickel and dime the customers through taxes and fees. Certain airlines impose a fee of $75 for booking award seats within 21 days of departure, and some airlines charge exorbitant surcharges, in addition to the miles for certain itineraries. In some cases, the surcharge can amount to as much as one third of the full fare. Furthermore, airline miles, with few exceptions, cannot be transferred to another account without a fee. Transferring miles to a spouse's or a friend's account on American Airlines, for instance, costs approximately $100 for every 10,000 miles. Note that these rates aren't for buying miles, but for simply moving the balance from one account to another! To put it in perspective, transferring 25,000 miles to a friend so that he or she could redeem a round-trip ticket within the United States would cost $250. You might as well as give the money to the friend and have them buy a revenue seat directly.

Having the miles is one thing, but some airlines make it criminally difficult to find seats that were available for redemption. Most airlines belong to one of three major alliances: Star Alliance, Oneworld, and SkyTeam. In principle, it is possible to use an airline's miles to redeem flights on their alliance partner, but good luck finding those partner seats if you haven't been through the mileage rodeo before. Some airlines don't even make certain partner flights visible on their search engine, though the situation has changed over the years. The most loathsome practice, one often greeted with wailing and gnashing of teeth, is the update of the redemption chart to require more miles per award seat. Known as "devaluation" in the airline miles community, these updates are universally detested since they essentially amount to a *haircut* in the savings balance of every single frequent flyer account. If the United States were to impose a levy or cut on bank accounts, people would be up in arms and there'd be blood on the street. And yet airlines do this without repercussion practically every year or so.

Let's trace the life of a typical credit card miles bonus, and we'll see how profitable the miles are. In a typical credit card application, the bank gives the consumer a bonus of 50,000 miles, which the banks bought from the airlines at a rate of, say, one cent each. Immediately upfront, the airline gets $500 in its bank account. Let's say that the 50,000 miles can be redeemed for $500 worth of service on the airline. This does not actually cost the airline $500 in future service, since the airline can (and does) control the supply of seats available for award redemption. An airline can drip-feed empty seats as it sees fit in exchange for mileage redemption with minimal impact on the revenue seats. Therefore, the cost for the airline to provide the award seats is nominal in comparison to the money received. Not only that, the consumer's stash of $500-equivalent airline services is in constant danger of being diluted, devalued, or expiring. The airline can (and some gleefully do) tack on surcharges, fees, and potential penalty to the award redemption to further recoup money from the award seat. If the consumer does not redeem or renew the miles within 18 months (or however long it takes to expire), then the miles disappear off the liability sheets, and the airline gets $500 free and clear. Furthermore, if the airline decides that it doesn't like the number of miles outstanding on its balance sheets, it could always devalue its outstanding miles with impunity.

When one sees it from the airlines' point of view, the frequent flyer program is probably the greatest commercial alchemy of the late twentieth century, and whoever invented the program should receive an economics medal from Stockholm. The airlines have essentially taken seats that were unsold and then peddled them to the general public for much more than the seat would have cost if bought in cash! And yet despite the inordinate disadvantages, people still flock to frequent flyer programs like moths to a light bulb. If there's a better way for a company to get money thrown at it without being named Apple, then I don't know it.

So, enough about how the airlines are holding the whip, blindfold, and handcuffs in this *Fifty Shades of Grey*-style relationship. Let's talk about how we can turn the table and be the one cracking the whip.

To begin, any game player needs to know the worth of a credit card application. My own personal rule is to apply for a card only if the rewards exceed $350, and it has served me well. Think about it this way. When you apply for a credit card, you're doing the banks a favor, not the other way around, and the banks have to compensate you properly for the favor. They aren't always honest with their compensation, though. You've probably seen credit card offers at department store checkouts for 20 percent off, or a discount of between $50 and $100. I've flown on airlines where the captain himself, no less, advertised for an airline card over the PA with 25,000 miles bonus (plus 1,000 additional miles for signing up in-plane). Low ballers, all of them! In my days I've seen card bonuses go as high as $1,000 per application, though $500 seems to be about the average. I only lowered my threshold to $350 because with my churning rate I'm practically scraping the bottom of the barrel.

For major airlines, the typical bounty should be about 50,000 miles per card application, though the rates could dip down as low as 35,000 miles, depending on the phase of the moon and planetary alignment. (For most airlines, a safe estimate of the value is one cent per mile, unless you're applying for SkyPesos, then all bets are off). Small airlines tend to offer smaller sign-up bonus. Hawaiian Airline, for instance, typically offer bonuses up to 35,000 miles only, enough for a round trip to Hawaii. Its big partner American Airlines, however, usually offers 50,000 miles per application, which are enough to book 1.5 round-trips to Hawaii. Or one could apply to British Airways, which also has a standard bonus of 50,000 Avios. Those are enough for two round-trips to Hawaii if one departs from the East Coast. Barring targeted mail offers, the way to get the best offer is to go to FlyerTalk (the de facto online gathering place of miles enthusiasts), where one can find a list of the best bonus offers from all airlines, hotels, and banks—complete with links and instructions, spending limits, and advisory notes on qualifying criteria (if any). Sometimes, the best offer might dip down to 40,000 miles on either American or United, and one nifty trick is to apply for the lower bonus card anyway. When the bonus inevitably returns to 50,000, simply send a secure message to Rewards Services and ask for a match.

An addendum to the rule above is to expect nothing less than 2 percent discount when making purchases on credit cards. Our choice to make card swipes has value, and we should be paid accordingly. Practically every single card I know gives at least 1 percent cashback, but these days 3 percent or higher cards are so easy to obtain there's no reason not to have one. Personally, I don't put up with anything less than a 3.5 percent discount whenever using plastic. Remember, there's two ways to use credit cards: the wrong way is to use a credit card if you have no money, and the right way is to use it if you want to make money.

An important corollary is to never, ever use an airline card (roughly 1 percent cashback) for everyday purchases unless minimum spending or a nominal purchase is needed to reset the mileage expiration clock. There really isn't any reason to leave money on the table. I once sat next to an older gentleman in Economy Plus who gleefully showed me his UnitedPlus credit card. "I've got the entire ticket free," he beamed. He was tall and looked the part of a business traveler, complete with buttoned-up suits and a tie. I inquired if he booked using a sign-up bonus, but no, he earned all the miles from everyday spending. I did a quick calculation in my head. The same seats, according my work reimbursement receipts, cost about $350, but it would take $25,000 in card spending to earn the 25,000 miles required for the award seat. I nodded politely at my seatmate but inwards I was shaking my head. If I had spent the same $25,000 with my 5 percent cashback card, I would have gotten $1,250! That's enough to book the entire trip in business and have the airline grovel at my beck-and-call instead of the other way around jostling in cattle class with miles.

The secret to making miles work for instead of against you is to neutralize the myriad unfavorable rules confronting consumers. This strategy requires a combination of careful planning, meticulously keeping abreast of the game, and setting the corresponding expectation. One is not likely to score a cheap award trip within weeks of the travel date when most seats are allocated towards revenue instead of award pricing. Most trips should be planned far in advance, preferably with great flexibility in scheduling. Holding a stash of miles in several different airlines is prudent; the chance of scoring a cheap award seat increases when one has options. Likewise, when travelers can choose which airline to redeem miles with, they can opt for the one with the lowest surcharges and fees. The ticking clock on miles could be extended with negligible cost by taking an Internet survey or buying an iTunes song through an affiliated shopping portal, or through transferring points (my favorite method) from bank loyalty programs. United MileagePlus, for instance, could be refreshed with transfers from Chase Ultimate Rewards; American AAdvantage with SPG points; and British Airways Avios with either Chase Ultimate Rewards points or American Express Membership Rewards points. And the yearly devaluations . . . well, one can always shake a fist at the airlines and swear to retire from "miles" altogether, or just roll with the punches. I think of it as a tax, though unlike government taxes, this airline "tax" doesn't buy me civilization. It doesn't even buy me as much as a stick of gum. Oh well, render unto Caesar what belongs to Caesar.

In my experience, airline miles have sweet spots—areas where the redemptions are maximally advantageous. Not all airline miles are the same; they differ in their coverage, availability, value in cents per mile, schedule, redemption rates, and most importantly ease of use. Some mileage programs are like race cars, some are sedans, some are all-terrain vehicles, some are minivans, some are monster-trucks, and then some are unicycles (cough, SkyPesos, cough). The key lies in using the right tool for the right job.

There are three main schemes for miles redemption: region-based, distance-based, and fixed-rate. United and American, for instance, use region-based cost charts that require a fixed number of miles depending on whether the flight is inter or intra-region. For example, on American a round trip within the United States costs 25,000 miles at the lowest redemption regardless of whether the flight was from New York to Los Angeles or from New York to Boston, and likewise round-trips from United States and Europe cost 60,000 miles at the lowest redemption rate regardless of the actual origination and destination cities within those regions. Long haul flights are typically the best use for these miles.

Distance-based schemes like that of British Avios, however, charge a different number of miles depending on distance travelled. It scales from 4,500 Avios for one-way trips under 650 miles to 20,000 Avios for trips between 4,000 and 5,000 miles. These mileage programs shine best when used for short-haul or intra-region flights like Los Angeles to San Francisco, Los Angeles to Hawaii, or practically anywhere from southeast United States to the Caribbean. Rounding out the redemption schemes, some airlines like JetBlue and Southwest use a fixed-rate chart where the miles have a fixed value between one and 1.7 cents apiece. Since these programs are fare-based, the mileage required fluctuates along with the cost of the seat, but in return there are no black-out dates and any untaken seat can be redeemed with miles. These programs are best if you need an award seat next week, or if you're only travelling within the United States.

Perhaps one of the best deals in award redemption is a trip to Hawaii from the East Coast on British Avios. While most airlines require about 17,500 miles for a one-way from continental United States to Hawaii, under the distance-based Avios program it is only 12,500 miles. The funny thing is that these Avios-booked flights are serviced by British Airways' partners, so the same seat to Hawaii on American Airlines can cost either 17,500 miles if booked with American's AAdvantage, or only 12,500 Avios if booked under its partner British Airways. Who can fathom the strange logic governing the convoluted world of airline alliances and loyalty program? I don't really care about the *why*, though. All I know is that these quirks are some of the most profitable redemptions and that Delilah now practically expects annual trips to Hawaii. My first trip with Delilah to the Aloha state was booked with 50,000 Avios and $22 in taxes and fees, and she liked it so much she decreed we would go back at least once a year. Good thing that's only one British Airways card application away. Easy peasy.

Another place where the short-distance redemption on Avios shines brightly is the Caribbean, which could be visited nonstop from major American cities on British Airways' alliance partners. On most major US airlines' region-based schemes, short hops to the Caribbean cost the standard rate of 17,500 miles per leg. On British Airways distance-based scheme, however, one could go from New York to Bermuda for a mere 7,500 Avios. Increase that to 10,000 Avios and a New Yorker could make a jaunt to Cancun, Sint Maarten, San Juan, Antigua, or St. Thomas. From Chicago or Dallas, one could reach San Juan, Montego Bay, or Cancun for 12,500 Avios or fewer. The mother lode of Caribbean redemption, however, is Miami, where the lucky resident could book a flight to any Caribbean island within 650 miles for 450 Avios, mere snack money in the grand scheme of miles. This is the frequent flyer version of Black Friday fire sales, except that these redemptions are available year-round. Considering that a typical credit card application garners about 50,000 Avios in bonus, residents in Florida could travel to the Caribbean round-trip five times on a single application! If I had lived in Miami, my dating life would have been so much easier. Imagine being able to say on the second date: "Honey, pack your bags, we're going to the Caribbean for the weekend," or on the fourth date, "Pick an island, any island."

For domestic (not counting Hawaii) travel, the absolute best deal I've found is the Southwest Companion Pass. The pass is valid for the remainder of the year in which it is earned, plus the entire year that follows. It allows the bearer to designate one individual as a companion. Whenever the bearer books a flight via Southwest, he or she can apply the pass, allowing the companion to fly along on the same route free of charge, regardless of whether the flight was booked with cash or with miles. To make the deal even sweeter, the pass can be used without limit as long as it remains valid. Earning the pass requires either taking 100 qualifying one-way flights with Southwest, or earning 110,000 Southwest points in a year. The latter route is preferred by card smiths as Southwest offers multiple credit cards. Most people I know get the pass by applying for two Southwest cards and pushing through $10,000 in purchases, which for the experienced card smith is the equivalent of a goal kick at the two-yard line.

It is possible to make the Southwest Companion Pass even sweeter by linking it with the Chase Ultimate Rewards program, which lists Southwest as a transfer partner. The steady supply of Chase UR points (thanks Staples), along with the generous redemption of Southwest, allows a traveler to experience the best of both worlds. Of course, the number of routes available on Southwest is rather limited in view of its comparatively small fleet, but this is more than compensated by the comparatively generous award program, which not only has no expiration date but also allows for the booking of any seats at a fixed-point-to-dollar conversion rate. I once did some calculations and found that Chase UR points and the Southwest companion pass combined equate to a perpetual 75 percent discount on Southwest flights. This is my preferred choice for domestic travel these days.

Usually, the best value for miles is reserved for international trips, where the cost could easily run into thousands of dollars. On most airlines, optimal domestic redemption usually produces a cent per mile ratio between one and 1.5. Internationally, optimal redemption can produce values in excess of two or three cents per mile, especially if one flies in business class. I once flew four friends and myself from Los Angeles to Washington, DC on miles. (Funny story: I was in the airplane unsuccessfully trying to blow air into my inflatable headrest, so I turned to Logan and said, "Can you help me blow this up?" The passenger in front of us swiveled around like an owl. He glared at us before relaxing his gaze on the deflated headrest. "That's the last thing you wanna hear on an airplane," he said.) That trip cost me 25,000 miles per person while the seats were going for $400 each in cash, so my redemption was worth about 1.6 cents per dollar. When Delilah and I went on our third European honeymoon, we booked flights from Los Angeles to Athens, Athens to Istanbul, and Pisa back to Los Angeles for a paltry 60,000 United miles. The same itinerary was going for $1,600 per person, so the redemption was worth 2.7 cents per mile.

On the topic of international redemption, one of my early-day frustrations was finding the darn award seats on partner airlines. Most airlines do fairly well when searching for award seats on their own routes, but when it comes to showing availability of partner airlines for international routes, the experience ranges from passable to spectacularly opaque. One workaround is to search for a partner's availability using the company's own search engine. A couple of years ago, I had a devil of a time trying to find tickets from Los Angeles to Hawaii using British Airways' search engine. The engine only showed three or four American Airlines award seats available for the entire month, even though I was booking six months in advance. Switching to American Airlines' own search engine, I found award seats on practically every day of the week, so I ended up noting the flight number and phoning British Airways' customer service to redeem seats. Similarly, flights into and out of Spain and Portugal on AAdvantage tend to be routed through London on British Airways, with very few flights being shown as operated non-stop by the alliance partner Iberian Airlines. The taxes and fees for stopping in

London on British Airways are quite onerous, amounting to as much as $300 per one-way leg, which explains why the British Avios program, like prophets of old, is held in high esteem everywhere but in its homeland. Here too, the workaround is to first check availability on Iberian search engines and then call into American Airlines' customer service with the flight number.

For trips to Europe, I have only used American and United miles so far, and I am happy with both of them due to the ease of earning card bonuses, generous inventory of award seats, and the fact that both programs can be topped up by transferring bank loyalty points (SPG points can transfer to American, and Chase Ultimate Rewards can transfer to United). American Airlines has an off-peak chart that lowers the redemption rate to Europe to 20,000 miles (compared with the typical 30,000 miles) per one-way trip between Oct 15th and May 15th. Care must be taken to avoid routing the trip through United Kingdom on British Airways, however. Other than that, AAdvantage generally has good coverage throughout most of Europe, especially if one needs to fly to Germany or the Iberian peninsula, which are served by American's partners, Air Berlin and Iberian, respectively.

Although United Airlines has occasional sales that are similar to off-peak pricing, it does not have a fixed off-peak chart. United's trips to Europe are fixed at a standard 30,000 miles per way in economy class. However, one great if mostly unknown feature of United is the free stopover (available only when booking international award round-trips). Defined as "an extended stay," meaning more than 24 hours, at an intermediate city between the beginning and ending city, a stopover is essentially a prolonged layover. Under the United program, it is possible to fly from city A to city B, stay over for as many days as desired, and continue on to city C. This counts as the outbound leg. The traveler could then fly home to A and the whole trip would still cost only 60,000 miles. It is essentially a free flight courtesy of United—fly two legs and get one free. When my friend Shawn was considering honeymooning in Japan, the going rate was 70,000 miles for a round-trip ticket at the economy saver rate. After some discussion, we constructed an itinerary in which he flew to Thailand first and spent a week-long stopover there. After that, he flew to Tokyo where he and his wife spent another week just in time for the national cherry blossom viewing festival. Flights from Bangkok to Tokyo were going for roughly $400 per person in economy, but he got two seats practically free.

I once read of a congressional attempt to regulate the frequent flyer industry. Not surprisingly, the attempt failed due to strenuous objections from both the airline industry and the travel hacking community. The article quoted a travel hacker who decried the attempted regulation as an example of the government poking its nose where it wasn't wanted. "If it ain't broke, don't fix it," the argument went. His defense of the status quo, its merits notwithstanding, was representative of the sentiments among the frequent-flyer community. An airline spokesman chimed in to say that they, God forbid, would not abuse their unconscionably-excessive powers and that the some people had been making a phenomenally profitable redemption on their miles program. Both groups agreed that the rules were fair. I remember shaking my head as I read the article. Life isn't fair, and those who say otherwise are already on the winning side. The people most vehement in protecting the status quo are always the ones who stand to gain the most from it. In this mileage game, the airlines and the travel hackers are the ones making out like bandits, with the typical consumers left holding the empty bag. If you ever apply for airline miles, don't be in that last category.

A section on miles basics isn't complete without mention of hotel loyalty programs. It's also a deep area of study, but you'll have to look elsewhere for a primer. Using hotel points is an art, but unfortunately I'm a science major. Hotel loyalty programs are generally affiliated with luxury brands, but Delilah and I have never been interested in staying at 5-star hotels, hobnobbing with aristocrats, or being pampered like royalty. Warm bed, clean sheets, hot showers: that's all we require in lodging and that's all we've looked for so far.

Besides, there's not a lot of money to be had in the arts anyways.

SOYLENT GREEN

IT IS A TRUTH UNIVERSALLY ACKNOWLEDGED that a manufactured spender in possession of a good workflow has a great support network of CSRs.

It was the week leading up to Christmas. Blue and green ornaments festooned Wal-Mart like little spheres of holiday cheer. It was impossible to turn on the radio or go into a store without hearing one or the other of the classical Christmas songs, which were getting a bit tattered around the edges from repeated use. Outside the store, bell ringers plied the ancient trade of wrangling peace on earth into goodwill towards men.

As a rule I try to avoid Wal-Mart during the holidays, when lines tend to swell to Depression-era soup-line lengths, and cashiers seem equally glum. Not much I could do about Christmas, though. Visiting any day of the week and any hour of day before the Big Day was like visiting a human-scale ant hill without the order and discipline. But the call of gift cards kept redialing if I didn't pick up.

My regular cashier Glenda was frazzled by the time I got some face time. The line behind me extended outside of the Money Center. Two other CSRs were manning the registers to either side while two more buzzed frantically in the back cataloging and shelving returns and exchanges. I proffered my credit card statements. "The usual, please."

We whirled in the familiar routine of the bill pay waltz. Glenda's hand flew over the keyboard with effortless ease, but her mind seemed disengaged.

"Busy day?"

She glanced up. The circles underneath her eyes seemed slightly dark. "It's been like this since morning."

About $4,000 later, I thanked Glenda and headed out of the Money Center. The line behind me had grown longer and more impatient. Overhead, a festive voice crooned the famous Christmas chorus, "It's the most wonderful time of the year." The writer of the song was obviously not into the cycling money. For us manufactured spenders, Christmas comes 13 times a year—once on December 25th, and once at the beginning of every month when our Serve monthly load limit resets. It's a mixed blessing. Twelve extra Christmases per year also mean 12 separate weeks before Christmas when, having already met the month's spending quota, we just sit around twirling our thumbs, restlessly waiting for Christmas Eve to come so we can commence opening gifts.

I still had $2,000 to liquidate, so I left the Money Center and, after picking up some groceries for Delilah, headed towards the check-out registers. Spying one on the far end of the room with a blessedly short line, I filed into queue. To kill time, I studied the cloud-based spreadsheet of my gift card activities from my phone. One should always have something interesting to read while waiting.

"Hello Jaime."

I looked up and saw Glenda. She had gotten in line immediately after me, clutching a Cheetos bag.

"First time I've seen you here on this side of the register," I said.

"Just buying my lunch."

I stole a glance at my cell phone. It was four o'clock in the evening. Calling it lunch would be stretching it.

"Isn't it faster to buy it from your register?"

"I'm on break. Can't do personal purchases while on the clock. Off the clock I can't touch the register."

"Sounds like a catch-22."

Her lips curved up in a ghost of a smile. "Company policy."

I offered to let her go first. The cashier gave Glenda a friendly nod and rung up the bag of Cheetos. "One dollar and ninety-nine cents," he announced. Glenda opened her wallet and after some consideration fished out a credit card. I knew by appearance most airline and worthwhile cashback cards, in fact, I knew the list so well that the only way to know it any better was in the biblical sense. But this card was entirely unfamiliar.

The cashier swiped at the register and, after an authorizing interval that seemed a bit lengthier than usual, handed it back. "Card denied, sorry." Glenda took the news in stride. She gazed at her wallet perplexedly, and then opened it once more and started thumbing through card after card, mutedly muttering to herself as she did so. Finally, she plopped one on the counter. "This one should work." I caught a glimpse of it as the cashier handed it back. A white activation sticker covered the front of the apparently brand new card, which was also one I didn't recognize. If it were anyone else, I might have thought him or her to be a card smith, but knowing Glenda I realized she was one of the many who played credit card hopscotch.

She waved goodbye and walked back towards the Money Center holding her newly purchased "lunch." I watched her amble away in her slightly hobbled gait, the view being occasionally obscured by a passing customer. In the distance, Glenda's white frazzled hair bobbed above her navy blue uniform like a lonely buoy in a sea of rowdy children and merry shoppers. Weariness swirled around her like an eddy. Overhead the PA crooned the lyrics to "Joy to the World."

Looking down at my cards, I had what I call a *Soylent Green* moment. It became clear who was really paying for all the easy travels and free-flowing cashback. It wasn't the large faceless corporations. It was Glenda and countless others who carry a balance on their cards, hopping from one card to another on borrowed time. Before this, I knew that card companies made money from balance interest, but the idea had the about same immediacy as the concept of mortality to a teenager. Now the truth stared at me face-to-face, with the haunting eyes of Glenda. It's a weird system, this whole credit card infrastructure. Unlike most other services, this one is funded through a punitive revenue scheme. The very usurious interest rate at which I scoff whenever applying for a new card is the same one funding my own cashback. Customers who pay off their card balance by the end of the month can use their credit cards free of charge; some, like me, even make out like bandits. The cost of the entire ecosystem (not to mention profit for corporate shareholders) is mostly borne by people who pay balance interest and punitive fees. Glenda, who worked long after her retirement age because she needed the insurance, had personally helped me liquidate almost $200,000 in gift cards. That's more money than most people have in their bank accounts upon retirement, and yet she helped me push that in less than two years to the tune of about $8,000 in profit. The other day she proudly showed me pictures of her grandkids, a boy and a young toddler, and I knew them by name. The thought that my own retirement and world travels were partially siphoned from her paychecks appalled me. Viscerally.

My mother's incredulous "Are they stupid?" question came back to me, and I couldn't resist shaking my head warily. Corporations are not stupid. They have orchestrated a massive wealth redistribution between two socioeconomic classes— those who need money and those who have money. The former class is heavily subsidizing the latter, funneling wealth upstream into the pockets of big executives and shareholders. Credit card smiths like me are tapping into the revenue streams like aphids diverting nutrients from a plant. What we consider good incomes are probably a mere drop in the bucket when it comes to institutional gross revenues.

Weirdly enough, in the enormous machinery of wealth transfer, there's an opportunity for a little piece of the American dream: the national ethos that hard work and merit are guarantees for a comfortable life. There's no culture more egalitarian than the credit world. Card corporations truly don't care about race, creed, gender, age, or sexual orientation. It doesn't matter if one is a brother, a queer, a bigot, a zealot, an aristocrat, or an octogenarian. These corporations are more than happy to issue a card as long as there is sufficient proof of income. They are equal opportunity blood-drawers. But they are also equal-opportunity bleeders. For middle-class people like me who use credit cards correctly, the Game guarantees a steady income and opportunities to visit the world if we are willing to put in the hours. To be honest, it's not easy work. One needs to have large tolerance for risk and rejection because the life of a card smith is truly one of rejection. If I had a penny for every time I heard, "Sorry, cash only," I'd probably have enough money for a McDonald's Happy Meal. And Wal-Mart . . . let's just say that loading cards at Wal-Mart is pretty much hit-and-miss, especially when loading at an entirely strange store. (One time an overzealous Wal-Mart employee even threatened to call the cops on me for suspected "structuring," but I stood firm in the knowledge of having done no wrong, and eventually he backed down). But like most other jobs, perseverance and networking eventually will lead to success. Unlike most jobs, however, the prospect of success is not complicated or thwarted by forces beyond one's control.

There are no ill-tempered bosses, discrimination, layoffs, or workplace politics haunting this dream. Card smithing is even mostly immune to the ebb and flow of economic cycles. In the good times, things are great, and in the bad times, things get even better as banks increase their card bonus to entice reticent consumers.

The gift card business isn't glamorous or easy, but it is (all things considered) honest work. It is veritably a small piece of the American dream, albeit one built from the cracked lives of many.

On the way out of Wal-Mart, I saw Glenda standing off to one side of the Money Center chatting with a fellow CSR, still enjoying what remained of her break. She held the half-empty Cheetos bag in her hand, occasionally offering it to her coworker. I paused for a moment and considered if I should give her a present. It was Christmas, after all.

I thought briefly of telling her about the Game. There could be no better present, but I eventually shook my head. My brother's words from long ago came back to me: "The Game is like fire. It can warm, but it can also burn." It is more than just a bag with a few tricks; it is a way of life—one that I was not then ready or able to describe properly. Besides, I wasn't sure Glenda was ready to hear about it.

I walked up to the counter. Glenda stopped her conversation and looked up. "Need anything, Jaime?"

I shook my head. "Just wanted to drop by to wish you Merry Christmas."

A smile cracked on her face like a sun peaking behind heavy clouds. I gave her a thumbs-up. "You're my number one CSR."

She brightened up. Her co-workers looked amused and somewhat envious. She came out behind the counter and gave me a genial hug. "Enjoy your holidays," she whispered. Her large hands enveloped me easily, and her perfume reminded me of my grandmother's.

231

THE PASSING OF OLD BLUE CASH

THE APOCALYPSE CAME IN WAVES.

It first started one Wednesday in late October last year (also known as Bloody Wednesday), when news came trickling in of Old Amex Blue closure. Some people were notified when their card suddenly ceased to work at the register, while many found the bad news in their email. It read, "You repeatedly used the Blue rewards feature of the card for purchases which are not consistent with personal, family, household use. Such purchases are ineligible for rewards under the terms and conditions of the card agreement." Ominously, the end of the missive stated, "Once a card is closed, rewards are forfeited."

The news caused widespread panic, and as closures continued in the following weeks denizens of the MS section of FlyerTalk hypothesized and debated the triggers for closures. The consensus was that Amex had finally noticed that the credit card with its unlimited 5 percent cashback was hemorrhaging cash and were identifying abusive cardholders through some set of unknown filters. Some suggested that possible criteria for termination included spending more than $50,000 per year, spending more than the stated annual income, having applied for recent Amex credit cards, having repeated purchases in multiples of $505.95, or cycling several times the credit line per month, but the continuing closure reports failed to provide any definitive answer. There just didn't seem to be any rhyme or reason to the way Amex constructed the filters.

Everyone dreaded checking email, fearing to see the infamous cancellation message. One poster had the scare of his life. "I found a message from Amex today with the subject heading: 'Information about your Blue Cash.' Nearly wet myself," he said. "Turned out they raised my credit limit."

Others dealt with the uncertainty with gallows humor. "It's like standing blindfolded on a firing line, and every so often you'd hear a shot ring out," one said blackly. As far as people could tell, the termination tended to cascade into closer inquiry on other cards held under the same identity. Some people with many Amex cards even considered pre-emptively closing their Old Blue Cash card as a firebreak. "My relationship with Amex is too precious to risk," wrote one of a recent voluntary closure. Many people immediately reapplied for the Old Blue Cash after getting the axe. A lucky few were approved. Most, however, were denied with the message, "Unsatisfactory prior relationship."

One recurring topic was finessing cashback from terminated accounts. The official stance, as stated in the Terms and Conditions, is that any outstanding rewards balance is forfeit upon closure. As many credit card smiths know, official company line is no hard impediment. In the beginning, many smiths attempted calling the Rewards department and, feigning ignorance, requested disbursement. It was an old gambit that took advantage of the fact that Loss Prevention and Rewards are separate departments and that in big companies "the left hand doesn't know what the right hand is doing." Sometime they were successful. Sometimes they weren't, at which point an application of the time-tested HUCA (Hang Up, Call Again) rule was in order.

Stricter enforcement of the company line soon stopped that stratagem, and some credit card smiths resorted to another gambit of torturing the logic of the terms and conditions. It revolved around the key passage in the terms and conditions regarding rewards: "Eligible purchases do NOT include purchases or reloading of prepaid cards, or purchases of other cash equivalents." One poster with four or five thousand dollars in lost rewards sent off a letter threatening legal action in small claims court, a copy of which he posted online. Crouched in quasi-legal languages, the crux of the argument was that gift cards were neither prepaid cards nor cash equivalents (haha), and even if they were, the long record of the company disbursing cashback for gift card purchases somehow formed an express modification to the contractual terms.

The poster's argument seemed to have the legal weight of a balloon, and the attempt to enforce it an ill-advised one. A competent legal department could easily countersue claiming that the cardholder had abused the system (not hard to prove with records of purchases in multiples of $500) and therefore had been unjustly enriched. If the company were to press for reimbursement of all rewards erroneously paid over the years (probably exceeding $50,000 for this particular card smith), then the poster would probably fold like a cheap lawn chair. After a while, his hawkish posts on FlyerTalk subsided and eventually ceased, and rumor had it that Amex settled and disbursed his lost rewards. A few other posters also reported favorable resolution for threatening litigation in small claims court. I guess I was wrong after all; for some people being wrong is no obstacle to winning.

As usual, the deductive and diagnostic posts were peppered with recriminations. Old timers sagely said, "I told you so," pointing to previous posts that the Old Blue Cash was too good to be long of this world. Light and moderate users blamed the heavy-hitters. How can this thing be sustainable when the whales were running $50,000 to $100,000 per month through it? Someone was bound to notice, they complained. The heavy-hitters in turn pointed their fingers at the bloggers for introducing the card to the masses. Widespread popularity was the card's undoing, not massive losses, they argued. Some newcomers who had just received the card lamented that they barely had any time to exploit it. "I only ran $40,000 through this card," one poster wailed. A few just laughed with merriment, saying things like: "Nothing lasts forever. F—- you buddy, I got mine." One or two fellows moaned the loss of their breadbasket. "Time to dust off the ol' résumé," they posted. All bemoaned the general decline of the Game.

Across the nation, spending on the Old Blue Cash nosedived like Egyptian stock prices after Moses summoned the Ten Plagues. The Eye of Amex was scanning ceaselessly, and no Old Blue Cash abuser, I mean *owner*, wanted to draw further attention to him or herself. The Blue Cash worked on a two-month reward cycle, so many were still waiting for the cashback from the previous two months to post. The writing was on the wall, but most hoped their precious accounts would last long enough to cash out one last time. I completely ceased gift card purchases on the Amex but continued making small purchases of groceries and gas in hope of fooling any potential scrutiny. Luckily, my statement closed on the 27th, so I immediately received one batch of cashback fairly soon after, after which I figured I was playing with house money. My brother wasn't so lucky. He had been spending $80,000 per month on the card, and his closing date was on the 20th, so the poor guy had to wait an entire month "in restless angst" for his $3,200 rewards.

As Thanksgiving approached, the general mood of the forum livened up. It seemed that we would have a few days' reprieve. It already had been a bloody month, and the decreasing rate of closure indicated that Amex was slowing down for the holidays. Many people had the 20th of the month as statement closing date, so when that date passed and the rewards posted there was good reason for cheers. Considering that Christmas was coming up, it seemed that most might limp on long enough to get the second batch of rewards. In the festive mood of Black Friday, Small Business Amex promotion, and Cyber Monday, some semblance of normality finally started to take hold.

The light at the end of the tunnel emerged in early December when Amex officially clarified the future of the Old Blue Cash through a modification of the offer page. Under the Rewards sections, it capped the total rewards annually: "You will receive 5 percent on Everyday Purchases up to $50,000." The glad tidings raced through the community bringing early cheer into the Christmas season. Many welcomed the news as an unexpected godsend because they had already written off the continued existence of the card. Having a cap of $50,000 a year certainly demoted it from mythical to merely legendary, but at least the card survived to continue its storied post in the toolbox of Manufactured Spend. Once again, Amex proved to be the corporation that kept on giving. Not everyone was happy, though. Some were apoplectic. "So emasculated it's almost useless," one poster wrote. Others were more practical. Their attitude was, "Not a problem. Just max out the spending in one month and then sock-drawer it the rest of the year."

Eventually the dust settled. Like survivors in an apocalyptic movie, card smiths poked out from among the rubbles, salvaged what we could, and went about rebuilding. My brother and I set out to reconstruct our workflow. The good old days of running a year's worth of Ivy League tuition through the Old Blue Cash each month were gone with the wind. My first priority was to acquire new Old Amex Blue. My wife's and mine survived the great purge intact, though they were now subjected to the annual cap. I was quicker and got to my mother first, from whom I got permission to apply for an Old Blue Cash in her name with me as an authorized user. In return, my brother reached my sister first, but fortunately I was right behind him.

"I'm borrowing your name for a credit card," he said one day at my mother's home.

She nodded. That may sound strange, but she and my brother Ben had become so inured to having their identities "borrowed," it was just another day in the Doughsmith household. I gave her a quick poke. "I know which card he's applying for." I winked. "Don't give it away. Rent your name out."

"I take it back. Now the name's for lease at $200 per year."

Grimacing, my brother protested. Feebly, though. I knew, as did he, that under the new cap the Old Blue Cash was still worth $2,500 a year in cashback.

"If he's not leasing your name, I am," I added helpfully.

Emboldened, she raised the stakes. "Okay, $300 per year for the name."

Harry hesitated. Fiona shot me a look to see if she had pushed the price too far. I surreptitiously pointed an index finger upwards in a gesture that meant, "Still room to go higher."

"Okay, final price: $400 per year." She turned to my brother. "Since you're the oldest, it's yours if you meet the price."

We got him on the ropes, though he was loath to admit defeat. Even at that price the Blue Cash was more remunerative than most and his decision was a foregone conclusion. Besides, I was ready to lease her name if he didn't, and he knew it.

"Forgot something important," Fiona added. "Cash only. No gift card, please."

I eventually managed to score yet another Old Blue Cash card for a grand total of four cards, guaranteeing 5 percent cash back annually on $200,000. A further $100,000 continued going through Staples and the Chase UR program. That left a gap of about a third of a million dollars that I needed to fill to restore my accustomed annual quota. Personally, there was something magically compulsive about the nice round figure of $50,000 per month. It's the minimum threshold for my gift card fix, below which restlessness starts to kick in. It was my Goldilocks number—not too little, not too much, just right.

My brother felt the same compulsion, but his withdrawal symptoms were especially hard because he was accustomed to a higher volume. Within months of the Great Old Blue Purge, he applied for a Wells Fargo card that offered 5 percent cash back on groceries, drugstores, and gas for six months. Soon he was running $50,000 through it per month. That was his nicotine patch.

Not surprisingly, the source of the next-best cashback opportunity turned out to originate from Amex. Known as the portal method, it required buying Amex gift cards through an online cashback portal, which gave a fixed percentage of the purchased goods as rebates for using an affiliated link. It's a bit convoluted, but it went like this. A card smith signs up for an account at an online cashback portal and then uses an affiliated link to buy Amex gift cards. Payment should be made with a card with at least 2 percent cashback. In addition to that base rate, the portal would also be giving an additional amount (typically 1.5 percent) for a minimum cashback rate of 3.5

percent. Not really a stroll in the garden, but beggars can't be choosers.

Funny thing, when I last looked at Amex gift cards from portals during the halcyon days of the Old Blue Cash, I thought I couldn't be bothered to engage such a tortuous scheme, with so many steps to keep track of: the delayed rewards from the portal, shipping dates, rolling 14-day purchase limits, and the constant danger of declined orders, just to name a few. A few weeks after the demise of Old Blue Cash, I found that I could indeed adopt Amex gift cards as my new favorite friends without a second thought—or even a first, really. It all comes down to motivation.

One amusing thing about these purchases that the mail carrier company Amex used had the annoying habit of occasionally dropping gift card envelopes at the doorstep if no one was home to sign. As far as I could tell, the consensus was that large purchases above $5,000 generally required a signature. Anything less than that and the package was liable to be left unceremoniously at the door. I've occasionally had as much as $4,000 in Amex gift cards (activated and ready for purchase) lying outside the door in a standard-sized white envelope just waiting for someone to come home from work. Anyone, and I mean *anyone*, could have walked up to my doorstep, collected the envelope, and walked away $4,000 richer, and my only defense against it was a nondescript envelope that obscured the true worth of its contents from the world. Security through obscurity was all I had. It's a recurring topic of angst for card smiths who are frequently absent from home during delivery hours. From experience, I can say that this method isn't for the faint of heart or the paranoiac.

Eventually a new workflow arose to replace the gap. It is not as remunerative as the golden days of yore; nothing could be. During a single month I push about $16,000 on the kneecapped Old Blue Cash (4 percent net). Another $8,000 goes through Staples (2.75 percent net), while $4,000 goes through reloadable cards (3.5 percent net). A further $22,000 is funneled through Amex gift cards at 2.3 percent net, with an extra $200 from online load and recurring banking bonuses rounding out the rest. Total monthly profit is $1,580, a step down from the previous $2,300 but still tolerable. I had previously managed to optimize my monthly time commitment to 30 hours a week, and now five extra hours of work are required to keep pace with portal-related bookkeeping, bringing my total monthly commitment to 35 hours. In terms of hourly rate, that works out to be roughly $45 per hour—a mere shade of the glory days, but still acceptable.

Life carried on in Manufactured Spend. Beyond the fact that the Old Amex Blue was no longer the mythical tool it once was, promotions and opportunities came and went unabated. In fact, one of the most generous limited-time promotions I'd ever seen came in the summer of 2015 when Amex offered an incredible deal of $25 statement credit per $50 purchase at Smart & Final stores, good for use up to three times. An easy $75 if one could find right item to purchase at Smart & Final.

I did a quick reconnaissance of the nearest Smart & Final when the news first hit. Right in the front of the central aisle was a gift card rack, on which Shell and Amazon gift cards were prominently visible. No gift card fees for either of those. This was so easy it was practically a giant bow-tied gift with the banner: "Amex loves you, card smiths!"

Sometimes big corporations are just too generous.

I was glad to see the offer, as was my brother. He had 18 separate cards that qualified. Together, Delilah and I scraped together 12 different Amex cards, which was not a difficult thing considering that authorized user cards and Serve Cards were also eligible. I busied myself visiting all stores within a 10-mile radius, cleaning out the shelves at each location. Each visit to the cash register consisted of three purchases of $50 each in gas or Amazon gift cards, which cashiers were happy to oblige without even batting an eye. I usually dread going to new stores to make large gift card transactions, as cashiers tend to look warily upon high hundreds or thousands of dollars in purchases—for good reasons, of course. Still, it felt good to blend in with a relatively unremarkable purchase. For once it was nice to make money without appearing shady.

One Saturday morning I sat in my mother's living room idly flipping through FlyerTalk to keep pace with the latest trends and rumors. The door opened and in swept my sister-in-law, hands full of grocery bags. She opened her purse and handed several cards to my brother. "I couldn't buy Shell or Amazon cards from Smart & Final."

"Why?"

"The shelves were empty. All cleaned out."

"Did you check the Smart & Final on Newhall?" he asked.

"Completely clean. And so's the one on Foothill."

Harry filed away the cards. "Awfully tough competition in this area," he mused.

The store locations registered in my mental map. "Don't bother checking the store on Bolsa," I said without looking up from my reading.

They swiveled and glared. "You're been to those places?"

I nodded, trying my best to suppress laughter.

Realization dawned. "You cleaned those places out?" she interrogated exasperatedly.

I nodded once more before bursting into hearty laughter.

She pivoted to my brother. "See what a monster you created?"

A few weekends later, I set out with the wife to finish off the remaining cards. Of my 12 promotion-eligible cards, four still remained. She wasn't keen on spending the weekend morning trekking to and from grocery stores. "Do I have to?" she groaned.

"No, you don't have to."

"Really?"

"But I'd hate to lose out on this free $300."

"Be right there."

By this time, the initial onslaught of card smiths had dwindled and my desired gift cards once more graced the rack. "Follow my lead," I said as we went through the check-out lane. I laid out $150 in gift cards in three equal piles. "Three different receipts, please."

The cashier nodded and within a few moments I was $75 richer.

Delilah followed suit, but she tarried a bit longer to make small talk. She had the perfect people skills to be a manufactured spender; she'd probably be one of the best if she ever joins the Game. God knows the sky is probably the limit for the amount that she could finesse through grocery clerks and Wal-Mart cashiers. Financial street smarts can be learned in a few weeks, but people skills like Delilah's either take years or winning the ovarian lottery. Too bad her interests don't lie on the pecuniary side of life.

I broke into a grin once we were outside the store. "That's the quickest $150 we ever made." She looked at the gift cards quizzically as if wondering why these companies were handing out money like Halloween candies.

At the next Smart & Final, Delilah went first in line. She divided the gift cards into three neat stacks, and on a whim added a small box of blueberries.

"Can I get these on three—"

"I know how this one goes," the cashier interjected. She was young, tall, and blonde. I wondered if she was a fellow card smith. "I didn't know if this deal was still on," she added.

"It's good until the end of the month," I replied. "You know of this deal?"

"There was a stampede last month. All gift cards were, like, gone within a week. One young guy, pretty shifty looking too, told me how it worked."

"I think there's still time to sign up an Amex card. You should register if you haven't done so."

"I did. I don't get the stampede, though. Nice deal but not that great."

Inside the car, Delilah opened the clam-shell box and started munching. "Nothing better than free blueberries." I reached over and fingered a few. "Yup, you're right."

She gazed out the window in a moment of reflection, "Three hundred dollars. Money's easy to make in America, isn't it?"

I held out one hand, palm down, and wiggled it back and forth to indicate "Just a little."

"This is fun." She picked up another blueberry. "Let's go to another Smart & Final."

I burst out laughing. "I'm out of registered cards. Money doesn't grow on trees, you know."

THE AGES OF CARD SMITHING

THE WEATHER, THOUGH IMPROVING, REMAINED COLD in the dying days of winter. Clump of trees stood barren in the parking lot. If one looked closely, little nubs of germinating leaves could be seen spouting from the end of branches like delicate tiny green ornaments. Occasional gusts kicked up brown dead leaves, and together they danced in an aerial ballet. Inevitably, however, the zephyrs faded and the leaves, having lost their dancing partners, drifted lifelessly to the ground.

I walked through the automatic sliding glass doors, where I caught sight of Maya working at the Money Center. That was odd. Glenda worked the Service Desk five days a week, Sunday to Thursday. I thought I had come on a Wednesday. Perplexed, I fished my cell phone out to check if I had misremembered today's date. It was really Wednesday.

I greeted Maya and handed over statements for credit card bill pay. "I thought Glenda is supposed to be on duty today."

Maya was a matronly woman with jet black hair neatly tied back in a pony tail. Her normal shift was complementary to Glenda's at two days a week—Friday and Saturday. She looked up from the card statement in earnest consternation. "She called in sick. I heard she was hospitalized."

"Is it something serious?"

"I don't know. I heard it has something to do with her kidneys."

"Do you know when she'd be back?"

Maya punched my credit card numbers in the keyboard, occasionally pausing to look down at my card statement. I've yet to see any CSR whose fingers can dance across the keypad like Glenda's. "No idea. For the moment I'm scheduled seven days a week."

The news hit me hard. In the previous week I had seen Glenda during my early morning run when she helped me load $2,000 onto the Serve and pay $2,000 to credit cards. She looked no different from normal. We joked about the cold weather and I inquired after her grandchildren. "Come visit more often," she said as I left.

I never saw Glenda again.

I miss her sometimes. We'd had a good run together. Through her hands alone I've probably done about a fifth of a million dollars, and she was one of the few cashiers who knew me by name. I still remember that one Christmas day when I stood watching her walk away in her slightly hobbled gait, clutching a bag of Cheetos for lunch and seemingly stuck in grim circumstances, while the world carried merrily on. Although I had seen her several times a week for the last two years, I didn't know where she lived or what her phone number was. I never thought of her life outside Wal-Mart, and now that she no longer worked at the store, the threads of our lives were separated forever. I wondered if she had gone to a better place.

I've done some thinking since then on the nature of the credit card business. The same credit cards that are the lifeblood of the Game draw sustenance from the lives of many who support the entire ecosystem through interest charges and a myriad of fees, some more defensible than others. When viewed from that angle, there's a *Soylent Green* feeling to it, but I prefer to think of the Game as a counterforce keeping corporate avarice at bay. In a way, card smiths keep card companies honest. If card smiths all disappear tomorrow, then at best the freed revenues would devolve back into the pocket of company executives and shareholders. I wouldn't bet the farm on them returning the money to customers by, say, lowering interest rates or extending payment schedules. A more likely outcome is that the card company, unimpeded by card smiths, would raise their perks and incentive schedules to entice fence-sitters who might not have gotten a credit card otherwise. By extracting steep gains from the card perks, card smiths force companies to walk a fine line between making competitive enticements and maximizing profitability.

We are market correction incarnate.

In the end, we're not saints fighting the good fight to protect the general credit consumers. God forbid, we're anything but our brother's keepers. Most of us are just looking out for ourselves, and anyone who says otherwise is kidding him or herself. The correcting pressure we happen to apply on big corporations is but a product of the ruthless efficiency of a capitalistic economy in which we are all but cogs and wheels.

One thing that all smiths pick up eventually is an appreciation for fleetingness of opportunity. Nothing last forever and no venue can be taken for granted. Promotions occasionally pop up for a week or so, some offers last only a few months, and even the reliable routes for churning money rarely last more than a few years. If card smithing has a coat of arms, it would be an image of two young boys sucking on the teats of a wolf, while the background would feature the gray silhouette of a cherry blossom tree. Green and blue are the heraldic colors—green for the grass and greenbacks, and blue for the sky and ocean. Like cherry blossoms, money smithing venues are transient, but are cause for pulchritude and celebration while they last.

Few are those who can peer far into the mist this landscape. There once was a time when people cycled money through the Mint, but those glorious days have long passed into legends. A few years ago, probably none could foretell of this Age of Wal-Mart and debit gift cards. And few can tell what Age will come after the current one passes into memory and folk lore. But we are a hardy lot. Constantly learning and adapting is the lot of all card smiths, for complacency and inflexibility do not survive long in this constantly shifting topography. The Hobby and the Game existed in the beginning when credit cards were in their infancy, and they will endure long after money orders and bill pays cease to be payable by gift cards.

When the twilight of the Golden Age of Wal-Mart passes away there will be a seismic shift in card smithing. There will be panic and upheavals, but if the past is any indication, that too shall pass. I know not whether the next epoch will be an Age of Iron or an Age of Heroes, but I know that I will still be shuffling money in whatever new venues that arise. And something will come along, I am sure of it. We are the manifestation of market arbitrage, constantly rushing in to take advantage of the price differences engendered by credit card perks and incentives. As long as card companies continue to offer enticement to entrap customers, card smiths will be there.

We will endure as long as greed abides in the heart of corporations.

EPILOGUE

DELILAH AND I WELCOMED A SON late in 2015. His name is Alex, and his arrival completely turned out lives upside-down. We had big plans to visit Belize, Hawaii, and the Florida Keys to snorkel all the great reefs, but Alex quickly put an end to that. We have no regrets, though. Feeling his little kicks through my wife's baby bump was more than enough recompense for missed snorkeling trips. It's exhilarating to be a father, but at the same time terrifying. Seeing him wrap his tiny hand around my finger and watching him smile in his sleep, I understood Scott Fitzgerald's ode to fatherhood,

> My heart is in the heart of my son
> And my life is in his life surely
> A man can be twice young
> In the life of his sons only.

Being responsible for another human being, much less one so small and helpless drastically changed my perspective on life. I've started taking notice of my shortcomings and making a conscious effort to correct them before Alex picks up on them. He's not yet at that stage, but it won't be long. One trait that has long dogged my days is absentmindedness, but I've never been motivated to address and overcome this shortcoming. Until now, that is. I've also never been a big recycler. To be honest, I never much cared for the state of the world years from now when I'm gone, but nowadays I try to sort out the plastics and bottles. These days the proceeds from gift cards are earmarked to Alex's college funds in addition to my vacation and savings account. Besides bankrolling my travels and retirement, Amex and Chase now have the honor of putting my kid through college.

For a while, I vacillated on whether to write this book. I've thought about what to teach Alex when he grows up. When he's old enough, I'll teach him the art of spotting frauds from gift card packages, and I'll let him unpeel and play with the empty cards. Once he enters boyhood, Delilah and I will take him abroad so that he can see the alternatives, good and ill, to the American way. When he's ready, I'll show him the Hobby and the way to fly the sky on someone else's dime. If he ever meets a special someone, I'll tell him about the "wings-before-rings" principle. I will train him in the Game so that he too can game the system.

The Game had been very good to me, allowing my wife and me to travel extensively at little or no cost while at the same time substantially padding our savings account. I used to be penny-pinching, excessively so, but according to my wife I've relaxed considerably since. Now, my favorite response to big unexpected costs or treats, whether it be a house repair or a dining splurge, is a shrug. "Oh well, it's only a few trips to Wal-Mart." And it's true. What my credit score has given me is an opportunity to acquire money on my leisure and mostly on my own terms. But the greatest gift I've received from Manufactured Spend is the opportunity to live a little wider, to see a little further, and to appreciate my wife a more fully. Never in my youth did I dream of visiting the likes of Paris, Rome, London, Florence, Venice, or Barcelona, let alone imagine a day when the only obstacles to jetting over the Hawaii for a week-long vacation are whether we have enough vacation hours and whether I can find two open award seats.

It's true that my wife and I have seen more of the world than many, and that's because we learned to stand on the shoulders of corporations instead of lying under their feet.

One thing that I've observed from my travels is that life is hard everywhere, but sometimes it is harder than it has to be. Many of the difficulties are unfortunately beyond control, but some of the most important are self-inflicted. When I survey the landscape of credit cards, I see three different classes of users: those who use credit cards because they don't have money, those who use cards but don't need money, and the card smiths who only spend in order to make money. The first class is massively subsidizing the other two, and the whole infrastructure is a system for redistributing wealth upwards from those who are least able to afford it. The one saving grace, however, is that membership in each of the three classes is entirely voluntary. Knowing that such a divide exists and that it is possible to move between the classes is half the battle.

The way I see it, it all comes down to two very basic concepts. The first is quite simple—if you're using credit cards because you don't have money, then you're doing it wrong. Such wanton usage is only going to increase the coffer of the big corporations and put some card smiths' kids through college. I know of a few people who treat their credit card as an access line to next month's paycheck, but that's only a medical emergency, a car accident, an economic downturn, or a surprise lawsuit away from the downward spiral of debt. It's like living in a house of cards, and the inevitable lot of those who live there is to inherit the wind. Mastering credit cards take discipline, and the first tenet is never to carry a balance. Get that down and one is well on the way to moving from the subsidizing to the subsidized user class. And trust me, the mastery is worth the effort.

The second concept is also simple—a good credit score is a terrible thing to waste. I can't help but cringe when hearing of people who wreck their precious scores though a forgotten payment, or who destroy their scores for a few quick grand. It's a terrible waste in the worst penny-wise, pound-foolish kind of way. A credit score can be a terrible burden, but it can also be a terrific birthright. One might view it as a shackle, but in the right hands it is a subsidy, one most generous. I think of a credit score like the trust in the Parable of the Talents in which a master gave his men money before leaving on a journey. The first two men put the money to good use and double their money, while the last one chooses to bury his for fear of losing it. Likewise, we're all entrusted with five talents, but while most are content to dig a hole in the ground and hide the money, some venture into the world and make five talents more. When it comes time for an accounting, those who buried their trust shall find their charges taken from them and given to the two who had ten talents.

It is my hope that writing about the secrets and the in-and-out of the Game will encourage more people to take a closer look at their finances and start asking new questions. Perhaps someone will stop asking, "What do I do with credit cards?" and wonder, "What can credit cards do for me?" Maybe someone, having read about the true worth of a credit score, will treat his or hers more gingerly. This game that we all play is a rigged game, but it's the only game in town. Perhaps someone will be motivated to look into what I call financial street-smarts and beat the companies at their own game. Practically everybody and their brothers know the price of credit cards, but very few know their value. I hope readers will realize that a credit score may be a necessary evil, but it could also be considered a harvestable good. In this game against the big banks, we've been playing with an ace up our sleeves all along.

I am aware that writing about the generous profits card smiths enjoy will have an adverse effect on the profession. Corporations are willing to accept a limited amount of loss from astute cardholders, and obviously the more card smiths there are, the less pie each person gets. But we all—interest-paying users, issuing banks, and card smiths—are tied together in an intricate weave of profit and loss. An increase in profit for the latter two can only come at the expense of the interest-paying cardholders, and conversely a decrease in revenue for the banks will lead to fewer profits for card smiths. Hopefully (and it's a big daring hope), as more people become astute about credit cards, there would be less revenue from interest charges; consequently, credit cards perks and incentives would dwindle. This would shift the status quo in a new direction, one not favored by card smiths. The profession will survive, though; it always does. What is bad news for the card smith community, however, is not necessarily bad news for everyone. A world in which the general card users can retain more of their income at the expense of multinational corporations is one that I, as a card smith, can live in.

It's a world that I want Alex to grow up in.

GLOSSARY

Amazon Payment: A peer-to-peer online payment service that allowed members to send money, fee-free, to others using a credit card. No longer available fee-free.

app-o-rama: The practice of applying for multiple credit cards within a few hours of one another to minimize impact of credit scores.

award seat: Airplane tickets that are booked with frequent flyer miles.

bill pay: A feature of online or retail services that allows a customer to transfer money from either checking accounts or debit cards to a creditor such as credit card, mortgage, or utility company.

card smith: One who engages in credit card smithing.

credit card churning: Applying for credit cards solely for the sign-up bonus.

credit card smithing: The art of refining perks, incentives, and rewards from credit cards.

cycling the credit line: Spending more than the credit card limit by sending in payments as soon as purchases post to the credit card.

debit card: A payment card that provides access to a stored-value balance (gift card or checking balance).

frequent flyer programs: Loyalty programs offered by airlines that allow a customer to earn miles (also called points) that could be redeemed for air travel.

gift card: Prepaid stored-value cards issued by retailers or banks that could be used for later purchases.

loading the Serve: Depositing money into the Serve Card at Wal-Mart's registers.

manufactured spending: Buying cash-equivalent products (gift cards) and using a credit card to earn points or bonuses.

air miles: Airline loyalty program currency that could be used to redeem for air travel.

minimum spending requirement: A specified amount of money one needs to charge to a new credit card within a set period of time (usually three months) in order to earn the sign-up bonus.

money order: A payment order for a specified amount of money, usually more trusted than a check because the funds are paid for beforehand.

PIN: Personal Identification Number, a numeric password that is required to authorize debit transactions.

points: The bank analogue of airline miles (e.g., Chase Ultimate Rewards, Amex Membership Rewards, Starwood's Preferred Guest points).

POS: Stands for point of sale, or the time and place where a retail transaction is completed.

revenue seat: Airplane tickets brought with money.

Serve Card: A prepaid debit account (think of this as a streamlined checking account) where money could be deposited at Wal-Mart's register using gift cards.

sign-up bonus: Incentives, or rewards for opening a credit card (e.g., 50,000 airline miles). A sign-up bonus usually requires a minimum spending amount within several months.

split payment: The process of dividing a transaction into several payment types or several cards (e.g., dividing a $2,000 transaction into four $500 payments).

swipe: The passing of a card through an electronic card reader.

Made in the USA
San Bernardino, CA
20 December 2015